D0217458

A
GRAMMAR
OF
SEPTUAGINT
GREEK

Frederick Cornwallis Conybeare, M.A., was elected Fellow of University College, Oxford, in 1880. He resigned in 1887 to devote himself to searching for and studying Armenian manuscripts of the Greek classics. This led him into the study of church history and the textual criticism of the Septuagint and the New Testament.

St. George Stock, M.A. Oxon., served at both Pembroke College, Oxford, and the University of Birmingham. He was prolific as a translator and editor of the Greek and Latin classics and as an author of works on theology and philosophy.

Both men were most productive as scholars in the decade or so on either side of 1900.

A
GRAMMAR
OF
SEPTUAGINT
GREEK

F. C. CONYBEARE
& ST. GEORGE STOCK

**ZONDERVAN**
PUBLISHING HOUSE OF THE ZONDERVAN CORPORATION
GRAND RAPIDS, MICHIGAN 49506

094138

A GRAMMAR OF SEPTUAGINT GREEK
Reprinted from *Selections from the Septuagint,* published in 1905 by Ginn and
Company, Boston, Mass. Zondervan edition 1980.

Library of Congress Cataloging in Publication Data

Conybeare, Frederick Cornwallis, 1856–1924.
   A grammar of Septuagint Greek.

      Reprint of p. 25–100 of the 1905 ed. of Selections from the Septuagint, according
to the text of Swete, by F. C. Conybeare and St. George Stock, published by Ginn,
Boston.
      1. Greek language, Biblical—Grammar.   I. Stock,
St. George William Joseph, 1850-   joint author.
II. Bible. O.T. Greek. Selections. 1905. Septuagint.
Selections from the Septuagint, according
to the text of Swete. III. Title.
PA717.C6 1980   487'.4   80-20829
ISBN 0-310-43001-1

Printed in the United States of America

83   84   85   86   87   88 — 10   9   8   7   6   5   4   3

TABLE OF CONTENTS

ACCIDENCE

CONTENTS

SYNTAX

GRAMMAR OF SEPTUAGINT GREEK

GRAMMAR OF SEPTUAGINT GREEK

ACCIDENCE

NOUNS, 1-14

1. Disuse of the Dual. The Greek of the LXX has two numbers, the singular and the plural. The dual, which was already falling into disuse in the time of Homer, and which is seldom adhered to systematically in classical writers, has disappeared altogether.

Gen. 40² ἐπὶ τοῖς δυσὶν εὐνούχοις αὐτοῦ. Ex. 4⁹ τοῖς δυσὶ σημείοις τούτοις.

Contrast with the above —

Plat. *Rep.* 470 B ἐπὶ δυοῖν τινοῖν διαφοραῖν. Isocr. *Paneg.* 55 c περὶ τοῖν πολέοιν τούτοιν.

2. Εἷς as Article. Under the influence of Hebrew idiom we find the numeral εἷς turning into an indefinite pronoun in the Greek of the LXX, as in Gen. 42²⁷ λύσας δὲ εἷς τὸν ·μάρσιππον αὐτοῦ, and then subsiding into a mere article, as —

Jdg. 13² ἀνὴρ εἷς, 9⁵³ γυνὴ μία. ii K. 2¹⁸ ὡσεὶ μία δορκὰς ἐν ἀγρῷ. ii Esd. 4⁸ ἔγραψαν ἐπιστολὴν μίαν. Ezk. 4⁹ ἄγγος ἓν ὀστράκινον.

There are instances of the same usage in the two most Hebraistic books of the N.T.

Mt. 8¹⁹ εἷς γραμματεύς, 9¹⁸ ἄρχων εἷς, 21¹⁹ συκῆν μίαν, 26⁶⁹ μία παιδίσκη. Rev. 8¹³ ἑνὸς ἀετοῦ, 9¹³ φωνὴν μίαν, 18²¹ εἷς ἄγγελος, 19¹⁷ ἕνα ἄγγελον.

Our own indefinite article 'a' or 'an' (Scotch *ane*) is originally the same as 'one.' We can also see the beginning of the French article in the colloquial language of the Latin comedians.

Ter. *And.* 118 f o r t e u n a m a s p i c i o a d u l e s c e n t u l a m. Plaut. *Most.* 990 u n u m v i d i m o r t u u m e f f e r r i f o r a s.

Apart from the influence of Hebrew, εἷς is occasionally found in good Greek on the way to becoming an article. See L. & S. under εἰς 4. In German the indefinite article and the first of the numerals coincide, and so a German, in beginning to speak English, frequently puts 'one' for 'a.' In the same way a Hebrew learning to speak Greek said εἰς ἀετός and so on.

3. First Declension. In classical Greek there is a tendency for proper names, especially those of foreign origin, which end in the nominative in -α preceded by a consonant other than ρ, to retain the α in the genitive, e.g. Λήδας, Ἀνδρομέδας, Κομπλέγας (name of a Spanish town, App. VI *De Reb. Hisp.* 43). In pursuance of this analogy we have such genitives as Βάλλας and Ζέλφας (Gen. 37²), Σουσάννας (Sus. O′³⁰).

On the other hand, nouns in -α pure, or -α preceded by ρ, are in a few instances found in the LXX to take the Ionic form of the genitive and dative in -ης and -η.

> Ex. 8²¹ κυνόμυιαν . . . κυνομυίης, 15⁹ and Gen. 27⁴⁰ τῇ μαχαίρῃ.
> i K. 25²⁰ αὐτῆς ἐπιβεβηκυίης ἐπὶ τὴν ὄνον. ii Mac. 8²³, 12²² σπείρης.

It is said that in the Papyri σπείρης is always used, never σπείρας. The plural of γῆ is found in the LXX.

> Acc. γᾶς iv K. 18³⁵. Gen. γαιῶν iv K. 18³⁵: Ps. 48¹¹: Ezk. 36²⁴: ii Esd. 9¹ and three other passages. Dat. γαῖς iv K. 19¹¹. γαίαις Dan. O′ 11⁴².

4. Second Declension. θεός has a vocative θεέ. Dt. 3²⁴: Jdg. 21³, 16²⁸: Wisd. 9¹. Usually, however, the nominative is employed for the vocative, as in —

> Ps. 21¹ Ὁ Θεὸς ὁ Θεός μου πρόσχες μοι · ἱνατί ἐγκατέλιπές με ;

But in Matthew 27⁴⁶ this passage assumes the form —

> Θεέ μου, Θεέ μου, ἱνατί με ἐγκατέλιπες ;

The Attic form of this declension is of rare occurrence in the LXX. λαός and ναός are the regular forms. λεώς does not occur at all, and νεώς only in Second Maccabees. ἅλως is common: but for that there is no non-Attic form, as it does not arise, like the others, on the principle of transposition of quantity.

5. Third Declension. The word σκνίψ (Ex. 8¹⁶) is interesting, as adding another instance of a noun-stem in -φ to the rare word κατῆλιψ and νίφα, which occurs only in the accusative in Hes. *Op.* 533. Σκνίψ is also found in the LXX with stem σκνιπ-.

6. Absence of Contraction. Many words are left uncontracted in the LXX which in Attic Greek would be contracted, *e.g.* —

Dt. 18[11] ἐπαείδων ἐπαοιδήν.　　Prov. 3[8] ὀστέοις.　　Sir. 6[30] χρύσεος.
Ps. 73[17] ἔαρ.

The accusative plural of βοῦς is always βόας, *e.g.* Gen. 41[4]. Similarly the accusative plural of ἰχθύς is left uncontracted wherever it occurs. Gen. 9[2]: Nb. 11[5]: Ps. 8[8], 104[29]: Hbk. 1[14]: Ezk. 29[4]. So also στάχυες, στάχυας, Gen. 41[5,7].

7. Feminine Forms of Movable Substantives. The form βασίλισσα for βασίλεια was not approved by Atticists. It is common in the LXX, whereas βασίλεια does not occur. *Cp.* Acts 8[27]. On the analogy of it we have Ἀράβισσα in Job 42[17 c], φυλάκισσα in Song 1[6]. The following also may be noted : —

γενέτις Wisd. 7[12] A, τεχνῖτις 7[22], μύστις 8[4].　　ὑβρίστρια Jer. 27[31].

8. Heteroclite Nouns.

αἰθάλη (Ex. 9[8, 10]) for αἴθαλος, which does not occur.

ἅλων (Hos. 9[2]), ἅλωνος (Jdg. 15[5]) for ἅλως, ἅλω. *Cp.* Mt. 3[12], Lk. 3[17] τὴν ἅλωνα. In the LXX both ἅλων and ἅλως are of common gender. Thus Ruth 3[2] τὸν ἅλωνα, 3[14] τὴν ἅλωνα : Jdg. 6[37] τῇ ἅλωνι : i Chr. 21[15] ἐν τῷ ἅλῳ, 21[21] ἐκ τῆς ἅλω. Josephus (*Ant.* V 9 § 3) has τῆς ἅλωος.

γήρους, γήρει for γήρως, γήρᾳ, but nominative always γῆρας. For γήρους see Gen. 37[3]: Ps. 70[9, 18]: but in Gen. 44[20] γήρως. For γήρει see Gen. 15[15], Ps. 91[15], Sir. 8[6], Dan. O' 6[1]. When one form is used, the other generally occurs as a variant. In Clement i Cor. 63[3] we have ἕως γήρους.

ἔλεος, τό for ἔλεος, ὁ. Plural τὰ ἐλέη (Ps. 16[7]). The masculine form occurs in some dozen and a half passages (*e.g.* Ps. 83[11]: Prov. 3[16], 14[22]). In N.T. also and in the Apostolic Fathers the neuter is the prevailing form, *e.g.* ii Tim. 1[16,18]: Tit. 3[5]: Hb. 4[16]: Herm. *Past. Vis.* II 2 § 3, III 9 § 1, *Sim.* IV § 2 : i Clem. 9[1], 14[1]: ii Clem. 3[1], 16[2]: Barn. *Ep.* 15[2]. In Mt. 9[13], 12[7], 23[23] the masculine form occurs, the two former being quotations from Hos. 6[6], where the LXX has the neuter.

ἔνεδρον (Jdg. 16[2]) for ἐνέδρα. The former is quite common, the latter occurs only in Josh. 8[7, 9], Ps. 9[28].

λύχνος, τό (Dan. O' 5[0]).

νῖκος, τό (i Esd. 3[9]) for νίκη. *Cp.* i Cor. 15[55, 57]: Herm. *Past. Mdt.* XII 2 § 5.

σκότος, τό for ὁ, occurs in the best Attic prose as well as in the LXX (e.g. Is. 42¹⁶) and in N.T. (e.g. i Thes. 5⁵). Cp. Barn. Ep. 14⁶, 18¹.

The N.T. and Apostolic Fathers afford other instances of hetero-clites, which do not occur in the LXX. Thus —

ζῆλος, τό (Phil. 3⁶: i Clem. 4⁸, ¹¹, ¹³, 6¹, ², 9¹, 63², but in 5², ⁵ διὰ ζῆλον: Ignat. ad Tral. 4²).

πλοῦς declined like βοῦς (Acts 27⁹: Mart. S. Ign. III εἴχετο τοῦ πλοός).

πλοῦτος, τό (ii Cor. 8²: Eph. 1⁷, 2⁷, 3⁸, ¹⁶: Phil. 4¹⁹: Col. 1²⁷, 2²).

τῦφος, τό (i Clem. 13¹).

9. Verbal Nouns in -μα. *a.* The abundance of verbal nouns in -μα is characteristic of Hellenistic Greek from Aristotle onwards. The following instances from the LXX are taken at random —

ἀγνόημα Gen. 43¹² (6 times in all).
ἀνόμημα i K. 25²⁸ (17 times in all).
διχοτόμημα Gen. 15¹¹ (5 times in all).
κατάλειμμα Gen. 45⁷ (20 times in all).
ὕψωμα . . . γαυρίαμα . . . καύχημα Judith 15⁹.

b. A point better worth noting is the preference for the short radical vowel in their formation, e.g. —

ἀνάθεμα Lvt. 27²⁸ etc. So in N.T. Acts 23¹⁴: Rom. 9³: i Cor. 12³, 16²²: Gal. 1⁸, ⁹. In Judith 16¹⁹ we have the classical form ἀνάθημα. For the short vowel in the LXX, cp. θέμα, ἔκθεμα, ἐπίθεμα, παράθεμα, πρόσθεμα, σύνθεμα.

ἀφαίρεμα Ex. 29²⁷: Lvt. 7⁴, ²⁴ etc.
ἄφεμα i Mac. 9²⁸. So κάθεμα, Is. 3¹⁹, Ezk. 16¹¹.
δόμα Gen. 25⁶ etc. So in N.T.
εὕρεμα Sir. 20⁹, 29⁴.
ἕψεμα Gen. 25²⁹ etc.
σύστεμα Gen. 1¹⁰ etc. So ἀνάστεμα. In Judith 12⁸ ἀνάστημα.
χύμα (for χεῦμα) ii Mac. 2²⁴.

10. Non-Attic Forms of Substantives.

ἀλώπηκας accusative plural (Jdg. 15⁴) for ἀλώπεκας.
ἄρκος (i K. 17³⁴) for ἄρκτος, which does not occur. Cp. Rev. 13² ἄρκου.
δῖνα (Job 13¹¹, 28¹⁰) for δίνη.
ἔνυστρον (Dt. 18³) for ἤνυστρον. So in Jos. Ant. IV 4 § 4.

ἐπαοιδός (Ex. 7¹¹) for ἐπῳδός, which does not occur.
κλίβανος (Ex. 7²⁸) for κρίβανος. So also in N.T.
μόλιβος (Ex. 15¹⁰), the Homeric form, for μόλυβδος.
ταμεῖον (Ex. 7²⁸: Jdg. 3²⁴, 15¹, 16¹²) for ταμιεῖον, which also occurs frequently. The shorter form is common in the Papyri.
ὑγεία (Tob. 8²¹) for ὑγίεια. In later Greek generally ὑγεία is usual, but the fuller form prevails in the LXX.
χείμαρρος (i K. 17⁴⁰) for χειμάρρους.

11. Non-Attic Forms of Adjectives.

εὐθής, εὐθές for εὐθύς, εὐθεῖα, εὐθύ, which also occurs frequently.
ἥμισυς, -υ is an adjective of two terminations in the LXX. ἡμίσεια does not occur. Cp. Nb. 34¹⁴ τὸ ἥμισυ φυλῆς Μανασσή with Jos. Ant. IV 7 § 3 καὶ τῆς Μανασσίτιδος ἡμίσεια.
χάλκειος, -α, -ον, the Homeric form, occurs in Jdg. 16²¹, i Esd. 1³⁸, 5 times in Job, and in Sir. 28²⁰ for χαλκοῦς, χαλκῆ, χαλκοῦν, which is very common.
ἀργυρικός i Esd. 8²⁴ only. Cp. Aristeas § 37, who has also ἐλαϊκός, σιτικός, χαριστικός (§§ 112, 37, 227).
αἰσχυντηρός Sir. 26¹⁵, 35¹⁰, 42¹ only.
σιγηρός Prov. 18¹⁸, Sir. 26¹⁴ only.
κλεψιμαῖος Tob. 2¹³ only.
θνησιμαῖος often used in the neuter for 'a corpse,' e.g. iii K. 13²⁵.

12. Comparison of Adjectives.

ἀγαθώτερος (Jdg. 11²⁵, 15²) is perhaps an instance of that tendency to regularisation in the later stages of a language, which results from its being spoken by foreigners.
αἰσχρότερος (Gen. 41¹⁹) is good Greek, though not Attic. Αἰσχίων does not seem to occur in the LXX.
ἐγγίων and ἔγγιστος are usual in the LXX, e.g. Ruth 3¹², iii K. 20². Ἐγγύτερος does not seem to occur at all, and ἐγγύτατος only in Job 6¹⁵, 19¹⁴.
πλησιέστερον adv. for πλησιαίτερον (iv Mac. 12³).

13. Pronouns.

a. Classical Greek has no equivalent for our unemphatic pronoun 'he.' One cannot say exactly 'he said' in the Attic idiom. Αὐτὸς ἔφη is something more, and ἔφη something less, for it may equally mean 'she said.' The Greek of the LXX gets over this difficulty by the use of αὐτός as an unemphatic pronoun of the 3d person.
i K. 17⁴² καὶ εἶδεν Γολιὰδ τὸν Δαυεὶδ καὶ ἠτίμασεν αὐτόν, ὅτι αὐτὸς ἦν παιδάριον καὶ αὐτὸς πυρράκης μετὰ κάλλους ὀφθαλμῶν.

In the above the repeated αὐτός is simply the nominative of the αὐτόν preceding. In a classical writer αὐτός so used would necessarily refer to Goliath himself. For other instances see Gen. 3¹⁵, ¹⁶, 39²³: Nb. 17⁵, 22²²: Jdg. 13⁵, ¹⁶, 14⁴, ¹⁷: i K. 17², 18¹⁶. Winer denied that this use of αὐτός is to be found in the N.T. But here we must dissent from his authority. See Mt. 5⁵ and following: Lk. 6²⁰: i Cor. 7¹².

b. As usual in later Greek the compound reflexive pronoun of the 3d person is used for those of the 1st and 2d.

Gen. 43²² καὶ ἀργύριον ἕτερον ἠνέγκαμεν μεθ᾽ ἑαυτῶν. Dt. 3⁷ καὶ τὰ σκῦλα τῶν πόλεων ἐπρονομεύσαμεν ἑαυτοῖς. i K. 17⁸ ἐκλέξασθε ἑαυτοῖς ἄνδρα.

So also in Aristeas §§ 3, 213, 217, 228 (ἑαυτόν = σεαυτόν), 248. This usage had already begun in the best Attic. Take for instance—

Plat. *Phœdo* 91 C ὅπως μὴ ἐγώ . . . ἅμα ἑαυτόν τε καὶ ὑμᾶς ἐξαπατήσας, 78 B δεῖ ἡμᾶς ἐρέσθαι ἑαυτούς, 101 D σὺ δὲ δεδιὼς ἄν . . . τὴν ἑαυτοῦ σκιάν.

Instances abound in N.T.

Acts 23¹⁴ ἀνεθεματίσαμεν ἑαυτούς, 5³⁵ προσέχετε ἑαυτοῖς.

c. A feature more peculiar to LXX Greek is the use of the personal pronoun along with the reflexive, like the English 'me myself,' 'you yourselves,' *etc.*

Ex. 6⁷ καὶ λήμψομαι ἐμαυτῷ ὑμᾶς λαὸν ἐμοί, 20²³ οὐ ποιήσετε ὑμῖν ἑαυτοῖς.

So also Dt. 4¹⁶, ²³: Josh. 22¹⁶.

As there is nothing in the Hebrew to warrant this duplication of the pronoun, it may be set down as a piece of colloquial Greek.

d. The use of ἴδιος as a mere possessive pronoun is common to the LXX with the N.T. *e.g.* —

Job 7¹⁰ οὐδ᾽ οὐ μὴ ἐπιστρέψῃ εἰς τὸν ἴδιον οἶκον. Mt. 22⁵ ἀπῆλθον, ὁ μὲν εἰς τὸν ἴδιον ἀγρόν, ὁ δὲ ἐπὶ τὴν ἐμπορίαν αὐτοῦ.

14. Numerals. *a.* δυσί(ν) is the regular form for the dative of δύο. So also in N.T. *e.g.* Mt. 6²⁴, 22⁴⁰: Lk. 16¹³: Acts 12⁶.

δυεῖν occurs in Job 13²⁰, δυοῖν in iv Mac. 1²⁸, 15². Sometimes δύο is indeclinable, *e.g.* Jdg. 16²⁸ τῶν δύο ὀφθαλμῶν.

b. The following forms of numerals differ from those in classical use: —

δέκα δύο Ex. 28²¹: Josh. 21⁴⁰, 18²⁴: i Chr. 6²³, 15¹⁰, 25¹⁰ ᶠᶠ. So in N.T. Acts 19⁷, 24¹¹. *Cp.* Aristeas § 97.

δέκα τρεῖς Gen. 17²⁵: Josh. 19⁶.

δέκα τέσσαρες Josh. 15³⁶: Tob. 8²⁰.　So in N.T. ii Cor. 12², Gal. 2¹. Cp. Diog. Laert. VII § 55.

δέκα πέντε Ex. 27¹⁵: Jdg. 8¹⁰: ii K. 19¹⁷.　So in N.T. Gal. 1¹⁸.

δέκα ἕξ Gen. 46¹⁸: Ex. 26²⁵: Josh. 15⁴¹.

δέκα ἑπτά Gen. 37², 47²⁸.

δέκα ὀκτώ Gen. 46²²: Josh. 24³³ᵇ: Jdg. 3¹⁴, 10⁸, 20⁴⁴: i Chr. 12³¹: ii Chr. 11²¹.

The above numerals occur also in the regular forms —

δώδεκα Gen. 5⁸.

τρεῖς καὶ δέκα, τρισκαίδεκα Nb. 29¹³, ¹⁴

τέσσαρες καὶ δέκα Nb. 16⁴⁹.

πέντε καὶ δέκα Lvt. 27⁷: ii K. 9¹⁰

ἑκκαίδεκα, ἓξ καὶ δέκα Nb. 31⁴⁰, ⁴⁶, ⁵²

ἑπτὰ καὶ δέκα Jer. 39⁹.

ὀκτὼ καὶ δέκα ii K. 8¹³.

ἐννέα καὶ δέκα ii K. 2³⁰ only.

c. The forms just given may be written separately or as one word. This led to the τέσσαρες in τεσσαρεσκαίδεκα becoming indeclinable, e.g. —

ii Chr. 25⁵ υἱους τεσσαρεσκαίδεκα.

The same license is extended in the LXX to δέκα τέσσαρες.

Nb. 29²⁹ ἀμνοὺς ἐνιαυσίους δέκα τέσσαρες ἀμώμους.

The indeclinable use of τεσσαρεσκαίδεκα is not peculiar to the LXX.

Hdt. VII 36 τεσσαρεσκαίδεκα (τριήρεας).　Epict. Ench. 40 ἀπὸ τεσσαρεσκαίδεκα ἐτῶν.　Strabo p. 177, IV 1 § 1 προσέθηκε δὲ τεσσαρεσκαίδεκα ἔθνη, 189, IV 2 § 1 ἐθνῶν τεσσαρεσκαίδεκα.

d. The alternative expressions ὁ εἷς καὶ εἰκοστός (ii Chr. 24¹⁷) and ὁ εἰκοστὸς πρῶτος (ii Chr. 25²⁸) are quite classical: but the following way of expressing days of the month may be noted —

Haggai 2¹ μιᾷ καὶ εἰκάδι τοῦ μηνός.　i Mac. 1⁵⁹ πέμπτῃ καὶ εἰκάδι τοῦ μηνός. Cp. 4⁵⁹.　ii Mac. 10⁵ τῇ πέμπτῃ καὶ εἰκάδι τοῦ αὐτοῦ μηνός.

VERBS, 15–33

15. The Verb Εἶναι. ἤμην the 1st person singular of the imperfect, which is condemned by Phrynichus, occurs frequently in the LXX. It is found also in the N.T.—i Cor. 13¹¹: Gal. 1¹⁰, ²²: Acts 10³⁰, 11⁵, ¹⁷,

22$^{19, 20}$: Mt. 25^{35}: Jn. 11^{15}. According to the text of Dindorf it occurs even in Eur. *Hel.* 931. It is a familiar feature of Hellenistic Greek, being common in Philo and Josephus, also in the *Pastor* of Hermas, and occurring moreover in such authors as Epictetus (*Diss.* I 16 § 19), Plutarch (*Pomp.* 74), Diogenes Laertius (VI § 56), Lucian (*Asinus* 46).

ἦς for ἦσθα, which is condemned by the same authority, occurs in Jdg. 11^{35}: Ruth 3^2: Job 38^4: Obd. 1^{11}. *Cp.* Epict. *Diss.* IV 1 § 132.

ἔστωσαν is the only form for the 3d person plural imperative, neither ἔστων nor ὄντων being used. This form is found in Plato (*Meno* 92 D). See § 16 d.

ἤτω for ἔστω occurs in Ps. 103^{31}: i Mac. 10^{31}, 16^3. So in N.T. i Cor. 16^{22}: James 5^{12}. *Cp.* Herm. *Past. Vis.* III 3 § 4: i Clem. 48^5, where it occurs four times.

ἤμεθα for ἦμεν occurs in i K. 25^{16}: Baruch 1^{19}. This form appears in the Revisers' text in Eph. 2^3.

16. The Termination -σαν. *a.* Probably the thing which will first arrest the attention of the student who is new to the Greek of the LXX is the termination in -σαν of the 3d person plural of the historical tenses of the active voice other than the pluperfect.

There are in Greek two terminations of the 3d person plural of the historic tenses — (1) in -ν, (2) in -σαν. Thus in Homer we have ἔβαν and also ἔβησαν. In Attic Greek the rule is that thematic aorists (*i.e.* those which have a connecting vowel between the stem and the termination) and imperfects take ν, *e.g.* —

$$\text{ἔ-λυσ-α-ν,} \quad \text{ἔ-λαβ-ο-ν,} \quad \text{ἐ-λάμβαν-ο-ν,}$$

while non-thematic tenses and the pluperfect take -σαν, *e.g.* —

$$\text{ἔ-δο-σαν,} \quad \text{ἐ-τί-θε-σαν,} \quad \text{ἐ-λε-λύκ-ε-σαν.}$$

In the Greek of the LXX, which in this point represents the Alexandrian vernacular, thematic 2d aorists and imperfects may equally take -σαν.

Of 2d aorists we may take the following examples —

εἴδοσαν or ἴδοσαν, εἴποσαν, ἐκρίνοσαν, ἐλάβοσαν, ἐπίοσαν, εὔροσαν, ἐφέ- ροσαν (= 2d aor.), ἐφάγοσαν, ἐφύγοσαν, ἦλθοσαν, ἡμάρτοσαν, ἤροσαν (Josh. 3^{14}).

Compounds of these and others abound, *e.g.* —

ἀπήλθοσαν, διήλθοσαν, εἰσήλθοσαν, ἐξήλθοσαν, παρήλθοσαν, περιήλθο- σαν, προσήλθοσαν, συνήλθοσαν, ἐνεβάλοσαν, παρενεβάλοσαν, ἐξελίπο- σαν, κατελίποσαν, ἀπεθάνοσαν, εἰσηγάγοσαν.

b. Instances of imperfects, which, for our present purpose, mean historic tenses formed from a strengthened present stem, do not come so readily to hand. But here are two —

ἐλαμβάνοσαν Ezk. 22¹². ἐφαίνοσαν i Mac. 4⁵⁰.

These seem to be more common in the case of contracted vowel verbs —

ἐγεννῶσαν Gen. 6⁴	εὐθηνοῦσαν Lam. 1⁵.
ἐπηξονοῦσαν Nb. 1¹⁸.	ἠνομοῦσαν Ezk. 22¹¹.
ἐποιοῦσαν Job 1⁴.	κατενοοῦσαν Ex. 33⁸.
ἐταπεινοῦσαν Judith 4⁹.	οἰκοδομοῦσαν ii Esd. 14¹⁸.
εὐλογοῦσαν Ps. 61⁵.	παρετηροῦσαν Sus. Θ¹².
ἐδολιοῦσαν Ps. 5⁹, 13³.	

Cp. Herm. *Past. Sim.* VI 2 § 7 εὐσταθοῦσαν, IX 9 § 5 ἐδοκοῦσαν.

Such forms occur plentifully in Mss. of the N.T., but the Revisers' text has only ἐδολιοῦσαν in Romans 3¹³ (a quotation from Ps. 13³) and παρελάβοσαν in ii Thes. 3⁶.

c. The same termination -σαν sometimes takes the place of -εν in the 3d person plural of the optative.

αἰνέσαισαν Gen. 49⁸.	θηρεύσαισαν Job 18⁷.
εἴποισαν Ps. 34²⁵.	ἴδοισαν Job 21²⁰.
ἐκκόψαισαν Prov. 24⁵².	καταφάγοισαν Prov. 30¹⁷.
ἐκλείποισαν Ps. 103³⁵.	ὀλέσαισαν Job 18¹¹, 20¹⁰.
ἔλθοισαν Dt. 33¹⁶: Job 18⁹, ¹¹.	περιπατήσαισαν Job 20²⁶.
ἐνέγκαισαν Is. 66²⁰.	ποιήσαισαν Dt. 1⁴⁴.
εὐλογήσαισαν Ps. 34²⁵.	πυρσεύσαισαν Job 20¹⁰.
εὔροισαν Sir. 33⁹.	ψηλαφήσαισαν Job 5¹⁴, 12²⁵.

d. In Hellenistic Greek generally -σαν is also the termination of the 3d person plural of the imperative in all voices, *e.g.* —

i K. 30²² ἀπαγέσθωσαν καὶ ἀποστρεφέτωσαν.

For instances in N.T. see i Cor. 7⁹, ³⁶: i Tim. 5⁴: Tit. 3¹⁴: Acts 24²⁰, 25⁵.

17. Termination of the 2d Person Singular of Primary Tenses Middle and Passive. In the LXX, as in Attic, the 2d person singular of the present and futures, middle and passive, ends in -ῃ, *e.g.* ἄρξῃ, φάγῃ, λυπηθήσῃ. The only exceptions to this rule in Attic are βούλει, οἴει, ὄψει, and ἔσει, of which the last is only used occasionally. In the LXX we have ὄψει in Nb. 23¹³.

The full termination of the 2d person singular of primary tenses middle and passive (-σαι), which in Attic Greek appears only in the perfect of all verbs and in the present of -μι verbs, as λέ-λυ-σαι, δί-δο-σαι, is occasionally to be found in the LXX in other cases.

ἀπεξενοῦσαι iii K. 14⁶.

κοιμᾶσαι Dt. 31¹⁶ (A).

κτᾶσαι Sir. 6⁷.

πίεσαι Dt. 28³⁹: Ruth 2⁹, ¹⁴: iii K. 17⁴: Ps. 127²: Jer. 29¹³ (A): Ezk. 4¹¹, 12¹⁸, 23³², ³⁴.

φάγεσαι Ruth 2¹⁴: Ezk. 12¹⁸.

So in N.T. —

καυχᾶσαι Rom. 2¹⁷, ²³: i Cor. 4⁷.

κατακαυχᾶσαι Rom. 9¹⁸.

ὀδυνᾶσαι Lk. 16²⁵.

φάγεσαι καὶ πίεσαι σύ Lk. 17⁸.

The *Pastor* of Hermas yields us ἐπισπᾶσαι, πλανᾶσαι, χρᾶσαι. Such forms are still used in Modern Greek.

In theory -σαι is the termination of every 2d person singular in the middle and passive voices, as in δί-δο-σαι, λέ-λυ-σαι, so that πί-ε-σαι is a perfectly regular formation. But in Attic Greek the σ has dropped out wherever there is a connecting vowel, and then contraction has ensued. Thus πίεσαι becomes first πίεαι, and finally πίῃ. Confirmation of this theory is to be found in Homer, where there are many examples of the intermediate form, e.g. ἀναίρεαι, δευήσεαι, ἔρχεαι, εὔχεαι, ἴδηαι, κέλεαι, λέξεαι, λιλαίεαι, μαίνεαι, νέμεαι, ὀδύρεαι, πώλεαι. It is an interesting question whether πίεσαι and φάγεσαι are survivals in the popular speech of pre-Homeric forms, or rather revivals, as Jannaris and others think, on the analogy of the perfect middle and passive of all verbs and of the present middle and passive of -μι verbs.

In καυχᾶσαι and the like, contraction has taken place in the vowels preceding the σ (καυχάεσαι = καυχᾶσαι). ἀπεξενοῦσαι (iii K. 14⁶) looks like a barbarism for ἀπεξένωσαι.

As against these fuller forms, we sometimes find contracted forms in the LXX, where the -σαι is usual in Attic.

δύνῃ for δύνασαι. Dan. O′ 5¹⁶. So in N.T. Lk. 16²: Rev. 2². In Eur. *Hec.* 253 Porson substituted δύνᾳ for δύνῃ, as being more Attic. δύνασαι itself occurs in Job 10¹³, 35⁶, ¹⁴, 42²: Wisd. 11²³: Dan. Θ 2²⁶, 4¹⁵, 5¹⁶: Bel Θ²⁴.

ἐπίστῃ for ἐπίστασαι. Nb. 20¹⁴: Dt. 22²: Josh. 14⁶: Job 38⁴: Jer. 17¹⁶: Ezk. 37⁴.

18. Aorist in -α. *a.* Another inflexional form for the frequency of which the classical student will hardly be prepared is the aorist in -α in other than semivowel verbs. Attic Greek offers some rare instances of this formation, as εἶπ-α, ἤνεγκ-α, ἔχε-α, and in Homer we have such stray forms as κήαντες (*Od.* IX 231), ἀλέασθαι (*Od.* IX 274), σεῦα (*Il.* XX 189). Nevertheless this is the type which has prevailed in the modern language.

b. In Attic the aorist εἶπα occurs more frequently in the other moods than in the indicative (*e.g.* Plat. *Soph.* 240 D εἴπαιμεν, *Prot.* 353 A εἴπατον imperative, *Phileb.* 60 D εἰπάτω, *Meno* 71 D εἶπον imperative).

In the LXX this aorist is equally common in the indicative.

εἶπα Dt. 1²⁰ : Ps. 40⁵.
εἶπας Gen. 44²³ : Judith 16¹⁴.   *Cp.* Hom. *Il.* I 106, 108.
εἴπαμεν Gen. 42³¹, 44²², ²⁶.
εἴπατε Gen. 43²⁹, 44²⁸, 45⁹.
εἶπαν Jdg. 14¹⁵, ¹⁸ : i K. 10¹⁴ : ii K. 17²⁰, 19⁴² : iv K. 1⁶ : Tob. 7⁵ : Jer. 49².
εἰπόν Gen. 45¹⁷ : Dan. O′ 2⁷.
εἰπάτω Dan. Θ 2⁷.
εἴπατε (imperative) Gen. 50⁷.   *Cp.* Hom. *Od.* III 427.
εἶπας Gen. 46².

c. While the classical aorist ἦλθον is common in the LXX, the form with -α also occurs, especially in the plural.

ἤλθαμεν Nb. 13²⁸.
ἤλθατε Gen. 26²⁷, 42¹² : Dt. 1²⁰ : Jdg. 11⁷.
ἦλθαν Gen. 47¹⁸ : Jdg. 12¹ : ii K. 17²⁰, 24⁷ : ii Chr. 25¹⁸ : Dan. Θ 2².
ἐλθάτω Esther 5⁴, ⁸ : Is. 5¹⁹ : Jer. 17¹⁵.
ἔλθατε Prov. 9⁵.
εἰσελθάτωσαν Ex. 14⁶.

This aorist is common in Mss. of the N.T., but has not been admitted into the Revisers' text. *Cp.* Herm. *Past. Vis.* I 4 § 1 ἦλθαν, § 3 ἀπῆλθαν : i Clem. 38³ εἰσήλθαμεν.

d. By the side of εἶδον we have an aorist in -α, especially in the 3d person plural, where its advantage is obvious. (See *h* below.)

εἴδαμεν i K. 10¹⁴.
εἶδαν Jdg. 6²⁸, 16²⁴ : i K. 6¹⁹ : ii K. 10¹⁴, ¹⁹.

e. Similarly by the side of εἶλον we have parts formed as though from εἶλα.

καθεῖλαν Gen. 44¹¹ : iii K. 19¹⁴.

εἵλατο Dt. 26¹⁸.

ἀνείλατο Ex. 2⁵.

ἀφείλατο i K. 30¹⁸.

διείλαντο Josh. 22⁸.

ἐξειλάμην i K. 10¹⁸.

ἐξείλατο Ex. 18⁴, ⁸ : Josh. 24¹⁰ : i K. 12¹¹, 17³⁷, 30¹⁸.

παρείλατο Nb. 11²⁵.

f. The aorist ἔπεσα occurs frequently in the 3d person plural, but is rare in other parts.

ἔπεσα Dan. O' 8¹⁷.   πεσάτω Jer. 44²⁰ (AS), 49² (AS).

ἔπεσας ii K. 3³⁴.   πέσατε Hos. 10⁸.

Among compounds we find ἀποπεσάτωσαν, διέπεσαν, ἐνέπεσαν, ἐπέπεσαν. So in N.T. —

ἔπεσα Rev. 1¹⁷.

ἔπεσαν Rev. 5¹⁴, 6¹³, 11¹⁶, 17¹⁰ : Hb. 11³⁰.

ἐξεπέσατε Gal. 5⁴.

Cp. Polyb. III 19 § 5 ἀντέπεσαν.

g. Other aorists of the same type are —

ἀπέθαναν Tob. 3⁹.   ἔλαβαν ii K. 23¹⁶.

ἐγκατέλιπαν ii Chr. 29⁶.   ἐφάγαμεν ii K. 19⁴².

ἔβαλαν iii K. 6³.   ἔφυγαν Jdg. 7²¹.

ἐμβάλατε Gen. 44¹.

h. The frequency of the 3d person plural in this form is no doubt due to a desire to differentiate the 3d person plural from the 1st person singular, which are confounded in the historic tenses ending in -ον. It also secured uniformity of ending with the aorist in -σα. In ii K. 10¹⁴ we have this collocation —

εἶδαν . . . ἔφυγαν . . . εἰσῆλθαν . . . ἀνέστρεψαν.

In Jdg. 6³ we find the anomalous form ἀνέβαιναν followed by συνανέβαινον.

19. Augment. *a.* The augment with the pluperfect is at times omitted by Plato and the best Attic writers. Instances in the LXX are —

βεβρώκει i K. 30¹².   ἐνδεδύκει Lvt. 16²³.

δεδώκειν ii K. 18¹¹.   ἐπιβεβήκει Nb. 22²².

δεδώκει iii K. 10¹³.   πεπώκει i K. 30¹².

ἐνδεδύκειν Job 29¹⁴.

So in N.T. —

δεδώκει Mk. 14⁴⁴.　　　　　　μεμενήκεισαν i Jn. 2¹⁹.
δεδώκεισαν Jn. 11⁵⁷ : cp. Mk. 15¹⁰.　πεπιστεύκεισαν Acts 14²³.
ἐκβεβλήκει Mk. 16⁹.　　　　　　πεποιήκεισαν Mk. 15⁷.
κεκρίκει Acts 20¹⁶.

But in the LXX we occasionally find other historic tenses without the augment, e.g. ii Esd. 14¹⁸ οἰκοδομοῦσαν. This is especially the case with εἶδον.

ἴδες Lam. 3⁵⁹.　　　　　　ἴδον Gen. 37²⁵, 40⁵.
ἴδεν Gen. 37⁹, 40⁶.　　　　πρόιδον Gen. 37¹⁸

b. In Attic Greek, when a preposition had lost its force and was felt as part of the verb, the augment was placed before, instead of after, it, as ἐκάθευδον, ἐκάθιζον, ἐκαθήμην.

The same law holds in the Greek of the LXX, but is naturally extended to fresh cases, e.g. to προνομεύειν, which in the Alexandrian dialect seems to have been the common word for ' to ravage.'

ἐπρονομεύσαμεν Dt. 2³⁵, 3⁷.　　ἠνεχύρασαν Job 24³.
ἐπρονόμευσαν Nb. 31⁹.

c. The aorist ἤνοιξα is already found in Xenophon. In the LXX it is common, though by no means to the exclusion of the form with internal augment. Besides ἤνοιξα itself, which is conjugated throughout the singular and plural, we have also the following —

ἠνοίχθη Nb. 16³²: Ps. 105¹⁷, 108¹.　ἤνοιγον i Mac. 11².
ἠνοίχθησαν Ezk. 1¹.　　　　　ἠνοίγετο iii K. 7²¹.
ἠνοιγμένα Is. 42²⁰.

So also in N.T. —

ἤνοιξε Acts 12¹⁴, 14²⁷ : Rev. 8¹.　διηνοιγμένους Acts 7⁵⁶.
διήνοιξε Acts 16¹⁴.　　　　　ἠνοίγη Rev. 11¹⁹.

Besides the Attic form with double internal augment, ἀνέῳξα, the LXX has also forms which augment the initial vowel of this, and so display a triple augment —

ἠνέῳξε Gen. 8⁶: iii Mac. 6¹⁸.
ἠνεῴχθησαν Gen. 7¹¹: Sir. 43¹⁴: Dan. 7¹⁰.
ἠνεῳγμένους iii K. 8²⁹: ii Chr. 6²⁰, ⁴⁰, 7¹⁵: Neh. 1⁶.
ἠνεῳγμένα iii K. 8⁵².

So in N.T. —

ἠνεῳγμένον Rev. 10⁸.

d. In προφητεύειν the internal augment is wrong, since the verb is formed on the noun προφήτης. In the LXX προεφήτευσεν occurs only in i K. 18¹⁰ (A) and Sir. 46²⁰. Nevertheless this is the form which has been everywhere preferred in the Revisers' text of the N.T.

προεφήτευον Acts 19⁶.

προεφήτευσε Mt. 15⁷: Mk. 7⁶: Lk. 1⁶⁷: Jn. 11⁵¹: Jude¹⁴.

προεφητεύσαμεν Mt. 7²².

προεφήτευσαν Mt. 11¹⁸.

e. Instances of double augment in the LXX are —

ἀπεκατέστη Ex. 15²⁷.

ἀπεκατέστησεν i Esd. 1³³.

ἠνωχλήθην i K. 30¹³. *Cp.* Dan. 3⁵⁰: Dan. O' 6¹⁸.

20. Reduplication. *a.* In verbs compounded with a preposition reduplication is sometimes applied to the preposition.

κεκαταραμένος Dt. 21²³: Sir. 3¹⁶. *Cp.* Enoch 27².

πεπρονομευμένος Is. 42². *Cp.* § 19 *b.*

b. In the form κεκατήρανται (Nb. 22⁶, 24⁹. *Cp.* Enoch 27¹,².) we have what may be called double reduplication.

c. With ῥεριμμένος (Jdg. 4²²) and ἐκρεριμμένην (Jdg. 15¹⁵) may be compared Homer's ῥερυπωμένα (*Od.* VI 59). ῥερίφθαι [ῥερῖφθαι] is cited from Pindar by Chœroboscus.

d. The reduplicated present ἐκδιδύσκειν occurs in four passages — i K. 31⁸: ii K. 23¹⁰: Neh. 4²³: Hos. 7¹. It is used also by Josephus. Κιχρᾶν, 'to lend,' occurs in three passages — i K. 1²⁸: Prov. 13¹¹: Ps. 111⁵. κίχρημι is used in this sense by Demosthenes.

e. The verb κράζειν has a reduplicated weak aorist, ἐκέκραξα, which is very common, especially in the Psalms; also a reduplicated strong aorist, though this is very rare.

ἐκέκραγεν Is. 6³.   ἐκέκραγον Is. 6⁴.

21. Attic Future. *a.* What is called the Attic future, *i.e.* the future out of which σ has dropped, is more common in the LXX than in Attic Greek. Thus the future of ἐλπίζειν, so far as it appears in Attic authors at all, is ἐλπίσω: but in the LXX it is always ἐλπιῶ. Among verbs in -ιζω which take this form of future are —

αἰχμαλωτίζειν	ἐγγίζειν	κερατίζειν	οἰωνίζειν
ἀποσκορακίζειν	ἐπιστηρίζειν	κομίζειν	σαββατίζειν
ἀφαγνίζειν	εὐαγγελίζειν	μελίζειν	συλλογίζειν
ἀφανίζειν	καθαρίζειν	μερίζειν	συνετίζειν
ἀφορίζειν	καθίζειν		

There is no apparent reason for the contraction in the future of verbs in -ίζειν. The retention of σ in the future of such verbs is quite exceptional, as in Eccl. 11⁴ θερίσει (mid.), Lvt. 25⁵ ἐκθερίσεις. Of the two versions of Daniel O' has in 4²⁹ ψωμίσουσι, while ℗ has ψωμιοῦσιν. Μηνίειν has a future in the LXX of the same sort as verbs in -ίζειν.

μηνιῶ Jer. 3¹².   μηνιεῖς Lvt. 19¹⁸.
μηνιεῖ Ps. 102⁹.

b. In Attic Greek there are a few instances of verbs in -άζειν dropping the σ and contracting in the future. Thus βιβάζειν, ἐξετάζειν have the futures βιβῶ, ἐξετῶ in addition to the full forms. In the LXX the former of these sometimes retains the σ in the future (Dt. 6⁷: Ps. 31⁸: Is. 40¹³: Wisd. 6³: Sir. 13¹¹), the latter always: but the tendency which they exemplify is carried out in the case of other verbs in -άζειν. Hence we meet with the following futures —

ἁρπᾷ Lvt. 19¹³.
ἁρπῶμαι Hos. 5¹⁴.
ἐκδικᾶται Lvt. 19¹⁸: Dt. 32⁴³: Judith 11¹⁰.
ἐργᾷ Gen. 4¹², 29²⁷: Ex. 20⁹, 34²¹: Lvt. 25⁴⁰: Dt. 5¹³,15¹⁹: ii K. 9¹⁰.
ἐργᾶται Lvt. 25⁴⁰: Job 33²⁹.
ἐργῶνται Is. 5¹⁰: Jer. 37⁸, ⁹, 22¹³, 41¹⁴: Ezk. 48¹⁹.
κατεργᾷ Dt. 28³⁹.
κοιμᾷ Dt. 31¹⁶.
κοιμᾶται Job 8¹⁷.

c. Both in the LXX and in the N.T. semivowel verbs, i.e. those with λ, ρ, μ, ν, have a contracted future, as in Attic, e.g. ψαλῶ, σπερεῖς, τεμεῖς, ῥανεῖ.

d. In Attic Greek the future of χέω is still χέω and indistinguishable from the present. In the LXX the future is distinguished by being treated as a contracted tense. Thus we have —

ἐκχεῶ,   ἐκχεεῖς,   ἐκχεεῖ,
ἐκχεεῖτε,   ἐκχεοῦσι.

The 1st person plural does not seem to occur.

e. To the contracted futures the LXX adds the post-classical ἐλῶ, from the same stem as εἷλον. This future occurs both in the active and the middle voices, e.g. ἀφελῶ (Nb. 11¹⁷), ἐξελεῖσθε (Josh. 2¹³).

So in N.T. —

ἀνελεῖ ii Th. 2⁸.

f. In Attic τελεῖν and καλεῖν are in the future indistinguishable from the present. In the later Greek of the LXX this ambiguity is avoided by the retention of the full form of the future. Thus we have—

	συντελέσω,	συντελέσεις,	συντελέσει,
		συντελέσετε,	συντελέσουσιν,
and			
	καλέσω,	καλέσεις,	καλέσει,
		καλέσετε,	καλέσουσιν.

g. The future ὀλέσω, which is common in Homer but rare in Attic, does not occur in the LXX, which has only the contracted forms—

ὀλεῖ Prov. 1³².   ὀλοῦνται Prov. 2²², 13², 15⁵, 16³³, 25¹⁹.

ὀλεῖται Job 8¹³.

h. On the other hand, ἐλάσεις in Ex. 25¹¹ is the only instance of the future of ἐλαύνω in the LXX.

i. In Attic σκεδάννυμι has future σκεδῶ, but in the LXX it retains the σ, *e.g.* διασκεδάσω Jdg. 2¹.

22. Retention of Short Vowel in the Future. As a rule in Greek α and ε verbs lengthen the vowel in forming the future. Exceptions are σπάω and χαλάω among α verbs, and among ε verbs αἰνέω, καλέω, τελέω. When the vowel is short in the future, it is also short in the 1st aorist.

To the ε verbs which have the vowel short in the future and 1st aorist we may add from the LXX πονεῖν, φθονεῖν, φορεῖν.

So in N.T.—

ἐφορέσαμεν . . . φορέσομεν i Cor. 15⁴⁹.

Cp. Herm. *Past. Sim.* IX 13 § 3, 15 § 6 ἐφόρεσαν.

23. Aorist of Semivowel Verbs. In Attic Greek semivowel verbs with ᾰ in their stem lengthen the ᾰ into η in forming the 1st aorist (as φαν-, ἔφηνα), except after ι or ρ, when they lengthen into ᾱ (as μιαν-, ἐμίανα, περαν-, ἐπέρανα). See G. § 672.

In the LXX many such verbs lengthen into ᾱ when the ᾰ of the stem is preceded by a consonant. Hence we meet with such forms as ἐγλύκανας, ἐκκάθαρον, ἐξεκάθαρα, ἐπέχαρας, ἐπίφανον, ἐποίμανεν, ἐσήμανεν, σημάνῃ, ὑφᾶναι, ὕφανεν, ὑφάνῃς, ψάλατε. In Amos 5² ἔσφαλεν is ambiguous, as it might be 2d aorist.

The form καθάρῃς is read in Dindorf's text of Xen. *Œc.* 18 § 8, and in Hermann's text of Plato *Laws* 735 we have καθάρῃ in B followed by καθήρειεν in D. The aorist ἐσήμανα is found as early as Xenophon. *Cp.* Aristeas §§ 16, 33. Ἐκέρδανα was always regarded as good Attic.

Such forms are also to be found in the N.T., *e.g.* —

ἐβάσκανεν Gal. 3¹.   ἐσήμανεν Rev. 1¹.

24. The Strong Tenses of the Passive. The Greek of the LXX displays a preference for the strong over the weak tenses of the passive, *i.e.* for the tenses which are formed directly from the verbal stem, namely, the 2d aorist and the 2d future. Thus ἠγγέλην, which is not to be found in classical authors, except in a disputed reading of Eur. *I. T.* 932, occurs frequently (in compounds) in the LXX, and the future passive, when employed, is the corresponding form in -ήσομαι, *e.g.* Ps. 21⁸¹ ἀναγγελήσεται, Ps. 58¹³ διαγγελήσονται.

So again from ῥίπτω we find only the 2d aorist and 2d future passive, *e.g.* Ezk. 19¹² ἐρρίφη, ii K. 20²¹ ῥιφήσεται.

The following are other instances of the same formation: —

βραχήσεται (βρέχω) Is. 34³.
γραφήσονται Ezk. 13⁹. *Cp.* Aristeas § 32.
διεθρύβησαν Nahum 1⁶.
ἐκλεγῆναι Dan. O′ 11³⁵.
ἑλιγήσεται Is. 34⁴.
ἐνεφράγη Ps. 62¹².
ἐξαλιφῆναι i Chr. 29⁴. *Cp.* Plat. *Phædr.* 258 B.
ἐπεσκέπησαν i Chr. 26³¹.
ἠκαταστάτησαν Tobit 1¹⁵.
ὀρυγῇ Ps. 93¹⁸.
περιεπλάκησαν Ps. 118⁶¹.
συνεφρύγησαν Ps. 101⁴.
ὑπετάγησαν Ps. 59¹⁰.

25. The Verbs πεινᾶν **and** διψᾶν. In Attic Greek these two verbs contract into η instead of ᾱ. In the LXX they contract into ᾱ, and πεινάω further forms its future and aorist in ᾱ instead of η.

ἐὰν πεινᾷ . . . ἐὰν διψᾷ Prov. 25²¹.   ἐπείνας Dt. 25¹⁸.
διψᾷ (ind.) Is. 29⁸.

The parts of πεινᾶν which occur in the future and aorist are πεινάσει, πεινάσετε, πεινάσουσι, ἐπείνασεν, ἐπείνασαν, πεινάσω (subj.), πεινάσωμεν, πεινάσητε.

So also in N.T. —

πεινᾶν Phil. 4¹².

πεινᾷ (ind.) i Cor. 11²¹.

πεινᾷ . . . διψᾷ (subj.) Rom. 12²⁰ (quoted from Prov. 25²¹).

ἐάν τις διψᾷ Jn. 7³⁷.

For the future and aorist of πεινᾶν in N.T. see Mt. 12¹,³, 25³⁵:
Lk. 4²: Jn. 6³⁵: Rev. 7¹⁶.

26. The Perfect of ἥκειν. Ἥκειν in the LXX has a perfect ἧκα,
which occurs however only in the plural.

ἥκαμεν Gen. 47⁴: Josh. 9¹².

ἥκατε Gen. 42⁷,⁹: Dt. 12⁹: i Chr. 12¹⁷.

ἥκασι(ν) 18 times.

This form occurs once in the N.T. —

ἥκασι Mk. 8³.

Cp. i Clem. 12² in a quotation from Josh. 2³.

The aorist ἧξα, which is found in late authors, is not used in the
LXX.

Wherever the form ἧκε occurs, it is either imperative, as in ii K.
14³², or imperfect, as in ii Mac. 4³¹, 8³⁵, 14⁴,²⁶.

27. Presents formed from Perfects. *a.* From the perfect ἕστηκα there
was formed a new present στήκω, which occurs in two or three passages of the LXX.

στήκει Jdg. 16²⁶.   στήκειν iii K. 8¹¹.

στήκετε (imper.) Ex. 14¹³ (A).

So in N.T. —

στήκει Rom. 14⁴.

στήκετε (ind.) Phil. 1²⁷.

στήκετε (imper.) i Cor. 16¹³: Gal. 5¹: Phil. 4¹: ii Thes. 2¹⁵.

στήκητε i Th. 3⁸: Mk. 11²⁵.

b. Similar to this is the verb γρηγορεῖν, formed from ἐγρήγορα. We
may conjecture that the pluperfect ἐγρηγόρει came to be regarded as
a contracted imperfect, and so gave rise to γρηγορῶ.

ἐγρηγόρουν Jer. 38²⁸.

γρηγορεῖν i Mac. 12²⁷.

γρηγορούντων Neh. 7³.

γρηγορήσω Jer. 38²⁸.

ἐγρηγόρησε(ν) Jer. 5⁶: Bar. 2⁹: Dan. Θ 9¹⁴.

ἐγρηγορήθη Lam. 1¹⁴.

From this verb in its turn was formed a new verbal noun γρηγόρησις Dan. Θ 5[11, 14]. *Cp.* also the proper name Γρηγόριος.

So in N.T. —

γρηγορῶμεν i Th. 5[6].

γρηγορεῖτε (imper.) i Cor. 16[13] : Mk. 13[37].

γρηγορήσατε i Pet. 5[8].

c. Of like origin is the aorist ἐπεποίθησα, which occurs in Job 31[24]. From πεποιθεῖν again we have the noun πεποίθησις iv K. 18[19].

d. The tendency to form new presents from perfects is already exhibited in Homer. Thus we have ἀνώγει (*Od.* V 139 *etc.*) formed from ἄνωγα, and γεγωνεῖν (*Il.* XII 337) from γέγωνα; also the imperfect ἐμέμηκον (*Od.* IX 439) from μέμηκα.

28. The Verb ἱστάναι and its Cognates. By the side of the forms in -μι there existed from Homer downwards alternative forms in -ω. Some of these present themselves in the LXX. Thus we have the following parts of the transitive verb ἱστάω.

ἱστῶσιν i Mac. 8[1].

ἱστῶν ii K. 22[34] : Job 6[2] : Ps. 17[33] : Sir. 27[26] : Is. 44[26] : i Mac. 2[27].

Among its compounds we may notice the following —

καθιστῶν Dt. 17[15] : Dan. O' 4[34]. *Cp.* Aristeas § 228.

καθιστᾷ . . . μεθιστᾷ Dan. Θ 2[21].

μεθιστῶν . . . καθιστῶν Dan. O' 2[21].

μεθιστῶσι i Mac. 8[13].

μεθιστᾶν iii Mac. 6[24].

So in N.T. —

ἱστῶμεν Rom. 3[31].　　　　　　συνιστῶν ii Cor. 10[18].

ἀποκαθιστᾷ Mk. 9[12].　　　　　συνιστῶντες ii Cor. 4[2], 6[4].

The form ἱστάνειν, also transitive, occurs in Ezk. 17[14]. *Cp.* Aristeas §§ 280, 281 καθιστάνειν.

So in N.T. —

μεθιστάνειν i Cor. 13[2].　　　　συνιστάνειν ii Cor. 3[1]. *Cp.* 5[12], 10[12].

Cp. Herm. *Past. Vis.* I 3 § 4 μεθιστάνει.

Later Greek has a transitive perfect ἕστακα, which is implied by the rare, though classical, perfect passive ἕσταμαι (Plat. *Tim.* 81 D). Thus in [Plato] *Axiochus* 370 D we find περιέστακας.

ἑστάκαμεν i Mac. 11[34].

ἀφέστακα Jer. 16[5].

καθέστακα Jer. 1[10], 6[17].

καθεστάκαμεν i Mac. 10[20]. *Cp.* Aristeas § 37.

So in N.T. —

ἐξεστακέναι Acts 8[11].

In Josh. 10[19] there occurs the irregular perfect imperative ἐστήκατε with connecting vowel α instead of ε. With this form may be compared πεποίθατε Ps. 145[3]: Is. 50[10]: Jer. 9[4].

29. The Verb τιθέναι and its Cognates. This verb does not offer much scope for remark. The imperfect is formed, so far as it occurs, from the alternative form τιθέω.

ἐτίθεις Ps. 49[18, 20].   ἐτίθει Prov. 8[28].

This is in accordance with classical usage, which however has ἐτίθην in the 1st person. Ἐτίθη is read by A in Esther 4[4].

The strong and weak aorists active seem to be about equally frequent. The only person of the latter that is missing is the 2d person plural. Ἐθήκαμεν is found (ii Esd. 15[10]: Is. 28[15]) and ἔθηκαν is common.

The 2d person singular of the strong aorist middle is always ἔθου, as in Attic.

In i Esd. 4[30] we find ἐπιτιθοῦσαν formed from the thematic τιθέω.

30. The Verb διδόναι and its Cognates. The present tense runs thus —

διδωμι,   δίδως,   δίδωσι,
                δίδόασιν.

In Ps. 36[21] we find 3d person singular διδοῖ from the cognate διδόω. The imperfect runs thus —

ἐδίδουν,   ἐδίδους,   ἐδίδου,
                ἐδίδουν or ἐδίδοσαν.

Ἐδίδουν as 3d person plural occurs in ii Chr. 27[5]: iii Mac. 3[30]; ἐδίδοσαν in Judith 7[21]: Jer. 44[21]: Ezk. 23[42]: iii Mac. 2[31].

The imperative active δίδου is found in Tobit 4[16]: Prov. 9[9], 22[26]. The 1st aorist is common in the singular and in the 3d person plural of the indicative, ἔδωκαν.

The 2d aorist subjunctive runs thus —

δῶ,   δῷς,   δῷ,
        δῶτε,   δῶσι.

Of the above forms only διδοῖ, 3d person plural ἐδίδουν, and ἔδωκαν are non-Attic.

The optative of the 2d aorist has the stem vowel long —

δῴης Ps. 84[7], 120[3].

δῴη 29 times. In Job 6[8], 19[23]: Sir. 45[26] δοίη occurs as a variant.
Cp. Aristeas § 185 δῴη.

So in N.T. —

δῴη ii Th. 3[16]: Rom. 15[5]: Eph. 1[17]: ii Tim. 1[16, 18], 2[25].

31. The Verb ἰέναι and its Cognates. *a.* The simple verb ἰέναι does
not occur in the LXX. It has therefore to be studied in its compounds. The regular inflexion of the imperfect in Attic is supposed
to be ᾖην, ᾖεις, ᾖει, though in Plat. *Euthyd.* 293 A we have 1st person
singular ᾐφίειν. Ἠφίεις therefore (Sus. O[53]) may be considered
classical.

b. The following two passages will set before us the points that
have to be noticed with regard to ἀφιέναι —

Ex. 32[32] εἰ μὲν ἀφεῖς . . . ἄφες.   i Esd. 4[7] εἶπεν ἀφεῖναι, ἀφίουσιν.

In the former of these ἀφεῖς must be from ἀφέω, a cognate thematic
form to ἀφίημι, but without the reduplication.

In the latter we have a new formation which treats the reduplication as though it were itself the stem. Of this new verb we have
the following parts —

ἀφίω Eccl. 2[18].   ἀφίουσι i Esd. 4[50].
ἀφίων Eccl. 5[11].

In the N.T. also we find ἀφεῖς (Rev. 2[20]) and ἤφιε(ν) (Mk. 1[34],
11[16]) the imperfect of ἀφίω. *Cp.* Herm. *Past. Vis.* III 7 § 1
ἀφίουσιν.

The weak aorist occurs in the singular and in the 3d person
plural ἀφῆκαν, *e.g.* Jdg. 1[34].

c. A thematic verb συνιεῖν existed in classical Greek. Theognis
565 has the infinitive συνιεῖν: Plat. *Soph.* 238 E uses ξυνιεῖς. Of this
verb we find the following parts in the LXX, if we may trust the
accentuation —

συνιεῖν iii K. 3[9, 11].   συνιοῦσιν (dat. pl.) Prov. 8[9].
συνιῶν ii Chr. 34[12].

So also in N.T. —

ὁ συνιῶν Rom. 3[11]. In Mt. 13[23] the R.V. text has συνιών.
συνιοῦσι (3d pl.) Mt. 13[13]: ii Cor. 10[12]

d. In addition to this we find a verb of new formation like ἀφίω —

συνίεις Tob. 3[8]: Job 15[9], 36[4].
συνίει Prov. 21[12, 29]: Wisd. 9[11].
συνίων Dan. ☉ 8[5, 23, 27] and *passim.*
συνιόντων (gen. pl.) ii Chr. 30[22].

In ii Chr. 26[5] συνιόντος and ii Esd. 8[16] συνιόντας the accent seems to be misplaced.

The new participle συνίων has not entirely ousted the -μι form in the LXX. We have συνιείς Ps. 32[15]: οἱ συνιέντες Dan. 12[3]: συνιέντας Dan. ☉ 14: τῶν συνιέντων Dan. 11[35].

e. The 3d person plural of the 1st aorist ἧκαν, which occurs in Xen. *Anab.* IV 5 § 18, is used in the LXX in its compound ἀφῆκαν.

f. The verb συνίειν is to be met with also in the Apostolic Fathers —

συνίω Herm. *Past. Mdt.* IV 2 § 1, X 1 § 3.
συνίει IV 2 § 2.
συνίουσιν X 1 § 6.
σύνιε VI 2 §§ 3, 6 : *Sim.* IX 12 § 1.
συνίων Barn. *Ep.* 12[10].

g. The 2d person singular present middle προίῃ in Job 7[19] is doubtless formed on the analogy of λύῃ, but might be reached from προίεσαι by loss of σ and contraction.

32. The Imperatives ἀνάστα and ἀπόστα, etc. It is the by-forms in -ω which account for these imperatives (ἀνάστα = ἀνάστα-ε). Ἀνάστα in the LXX is used interchangeably with ἀνάστηθι. Thus in Dan. 7[5] Ο′ has ἀνάστα, while ☉ has ἀνάστηθι. But the same writer even will go from one to the other. Thus in iii K. 19 we have ἀνάστηθι in v. 5 and ἀνάστα in v. 7, and again in iii K. 20 ἀνάστα in v. 15 and ἀνάστηθι in v. 18. So also Ps. 43[24, 27] ἀνάστηθι . . . ἀνάστα. Ἀπόστα occurs in Job 7[16], 14[6], 21[14].

So in N.T., where we find in addition the 3d person singular and the 2d person plural.

ἀνάστα Acts 12[7]: Eph. 5[14].   καταβάτω Mt. 27[42].
ἀνάβα Rev. 4[1].   ἀναβάτε Rev. 11[12].

Cp. Herm. *Past. Mdt.* VI 2 §§ 6, 7 ἀπόστα . . . ἀπόστηθι, *Vis.* 2 § 8 ἀντίστα.

Similar forms are to be found even in the Attic drama and earlier.

ἔμβα Eur. *Elec.* 113 : Ar. *Ran.* 377.

ἐπίβα Theognis 845.

ἔσβα Eur. *Phœn.* 193.

κατάβα Ar. *Ran.* 35, *Vesp.* 979.

πρόβα Eur. *Alc.* 872 : Ar. *Ach.* 262.

33. Special Forms of Verbs.

αἱρετίζειν denominative from αἱρετός.

ἀμφιάζειν iv K. 17⁹ : Job 29¹⁴, 31¹⁹ (in 40⁵ ἀμφίεσαι) = ἀμφιεννύναι.

ἀποκτέννειν Ex. 4²³ : ii K. 4¹² : iv K. 17²⁵ : Ps. 77³⁴, 100⁸ : Wisd. 16¹⁴ : Hab. 1¹⁷ : Is. 66³ : Dan. ☉ 2¹³ : iii Mac. 7¹⁴.

ἀποτιννύειν Gen. 31³⁹ : Ps. 68⁵ : Sir. 20¹².

ἐλεᾶν for ἐλεεῖν. Ps. 36²⁶, 114⁶ : Prov. 13⁹, 14²¹,³¹, 21²⁶, 28⁸ : Sir. 18¹⁴ : Tobit 13² : iv Mac. 6¹², 9³. So in N.T., Jude²²,²³. *Cp.* i Clem. 13² : Barn. Ep. 20².

ἐλούσθης Ezk. 16⁴.

ἑόρακας ii K. 18¹¹. Maintained by some to be the true Attic form.

ἐρρηγώς for ἐρρωγώς. Job 32¹⁹.

ἔσθειν for ἐσθίειν. Lvt. 7¹⁵, 11³⁴, 17¹⁰, 19⁸,²⁶ : Sir. 20¹⁶. Old poetic form. Hom. *Il.* XXIV 415 : *Od.* IX 479, X 273.

κάθου for κάθησο. Gen. 38¹¹ : Jdg. 17¹⁰ : Ruth 3¹⁸ : i K. 1²³, 22⁵,²³ : iv K. 2²,⁴,⁶ : Ps. 109¹ : Sir. 9⁷. Formed on the analogy of λύου. Κάθησο itself occurs in ii Chr. 25¹⁹. In Ezk. 23⁴¹ we have imperfect ἐκάθου. So in N.T., Mt. 22⁴⁴ : Mk. 12³⁶ : Lk. 20⁴² : Acts 2³⁴ : Hb. 1¹³ (all quotations from Ps. 109¹) : James 2³.

μαιμάσσειν Jer. 4¹⁹.

οἶσθας Dt. 9². Cp. Eur. *Ion* 999 (Dindorf).

πιάζειν for πιέζειν. Song 2¹⁵ : Sir. 23²¹. Πιέζειν occurs only in Micah 6¹⁵ in the original sense of ' to press.'

ῥάσσειν Jer. 23³⁹ and eight other passages.

34. Adverbs.

Hellenistic Greek supplied the missing adverb to ἀγαθός. Ἀγαθῶς occurs in Aristotle *Rh.* II 11 § 1. In the LXX it is found in i K. 20⁷ : iv K. 11¹⁸ : Tob. 13¹⁰.

Among adverbs of time we may notice ἐκ πρωίθεν and ἀπὸ πρωίθεν as peculiar to the LXX. For the former see ii K. 2²⁷ : iii K. 18²⁶ : i Mac. 10⁸⁰ ; for the latter Ex. 18¹³,¹⁴ : Ruth 2⁷ : Job 4²⁰ : Sir. 18²⁶ : i Mac. 9¹³. Similar to these among adverbs of place is ἀπὸ μακρόθεν, Ps. 138². Such expressions remind us of our own double form 'from whence,' which purists condemn.

In the Greek of the LXX ποῦ is used for ποῖ, just as we commonly say 'where' for 'whither.'

Jdg. 19¹⁷ Ποῦ πορεύῃ, καὶ πόθεν ἔρχῃ;

Cp. Gen. 37³¹ : Josh. 2⁵, 8¹⁰ : Jdg. 19¹⁷ : i K. 10¹⁴ : Zech. 2².

Ποῖ occurs only in a doubtful reading in Jer. 2²⁸, and has there the sense of ποῦ.

Similarly οὗ is used for οἷ, which is not found at all.

Jer. 51³⁵ οὗ ἐὰν βαδίσῃς ἐκεῖ.

Cp. Gen. 40³ : Ex. 21¹³ : iii K. 18¹⁰ : Ezk. 12¹⁶.
So in N.T. —

ποῦ = ποῖ i Jn. 2¹¹, 3⁸, 8¹⁴ : Hb. 11⁸.
ὅπου = ὅποι James 3⁴.

ὅποι does not occur in Biblical Greek.

35. Homerisms. The Ionic infusion which is observable in the Greek of the LXX may possibly be due to the use of Homer as a schoolbook in Alexandria. This would be a *vera causa* in accounting for such stray Ionisms as κυνομυίης, μαχαίρῃ, ἐπιβεβηκυίης, and the use of σπείρης in the Papyri; possibly also for γαιῶν, γαίαις. Such forms also as ἐπαοιδός, ἔσθειν, ἐτάνυσαν (Sir. 43¹²), μόλιβος, χάλκειος, χείμαρρος, πολεμιστής, have an Homeric ring about them.

36. Movable Consonants. ν ἐφελκυστικόν is freely employed before consonants, as in Gen. 31¹⁵, 41⁵⁵ : Dt. 19¹ : Ruth 2³ : Jdg. 16¹¹.

To ἄχρι and μέχρι ς is sometimes appended before a vowel and sometimes not.

Jdg. 11³³ ἄχρις Ἄρνων.	Josh. 4²³ μέχρις οὗ.
Job 32¹¹ ἄχρι οὗ.	i Esd. 1⁵⁴ μέχρις οὗ.
ii Mac. 14¹⁵ ἄχρι αἰῶνος.	Job 32¹² μέχρι ὑμῶν.

Ἀντικρύ and ἄντικρυς differ from one another by more than the σ. The former does not occur at all in the LXX, the latter in Swete's text only once, iii Mac. 5¹⁶ ἄντικρυς ἀνακλιθῆναι αὐτοῦ.

In the Revisers' text of the N.T. we find ἄχρι before a consonant in Gal. 4² ; ἄχρις οὗ i Cor. 11²⁶, 15²⁵ : Gal. 3¹⁹, 4¹⁹ : Hb. 3¹³ ; μέχρις οὗ Mk. 13³⁰ ; μέχρις αἵματος Hb. 12⁴ ; ἀντικρὺ Χίου Acts 20¹⁵.

37. Spelling. In matters of spelling Dr. Swete's text appears to reflect variations in the Mss.

a. The diphthong ει is often replaced by ι, as in i Esd. 1¹¹ χαλκίοις compared with ii Chr. 35¹³ χαλκείοις. This is especially the case with feminine nouns in -εία, as

ἀπωλία, δουλία, λατρία, πλινθία, συγγενία, ὑγία, φαρμακία.

Neuters plural in -εία also sometimes end in -ια with recession of accent, as —

ἄγγια Gen. 42²⁵. πόρια Gen. 45¹⁷.

In the pluperfect of ἵστημι again we sometimes find ι for ει —

ἱστήκει Jdg. 16²⁹. ἐφιστήκει Nb. 23⁶, ¹⁷.

παριστήκει Gen. 45¹.

So also in the future and 1st aorist of λείχω, as —

ἐκλίξει, ἐκλίξαι, ἔλιξαν, λίξουσιν.

On the other hand εἰδέαι for ἰδέαι (nom. pl. of ἰδέα) occurs in Dan. Θ 1¹³.

b. ν in composition is sometimes changed into μ before a labial and sometimes not, as —

συμβιβάσω Ex. 4¹². συνβιβασάτω Jdg. 13⁸.

Before a guttural or π, ν is often retained, instead of being turned into γ, as —

ἐνκάθηται, ἐνκρατεῖς, ἐνκρούσῃς, ἐνκρυφίας, ἐνποίῃ, ἐνχωρίῳ.

But on the other hand —

σύγκρισις, συγγενία.

c. In the spelling of λαμβάνειν μ appears in parts not formed from the present stem, as —

λήμψομαι, λήμψῃ, λήμψεσθε, ἐλήμφθη, καταλήμψῃ.

This may indicate that the syllable in which the μ occurs was pronounced with β. In modern Greek μπ stands for *b*, and we seem to find this usage as early as Hermas (*Vis.* III 1 § 4), who represents the Latin *subsellium* by συμψέλιον. *Cp.* Ἀμβακούμ for *Habakkuk*.

d. The doubling of ρ in the augment of verbs is often neglected, as —

ἐξερίφησαν, ἔρανεν, ἐράπιζον, ἔριψεν.

e. The following also may be noticed —

ἐραυνᾶν for ἐρευνᾶν Dt. 13¹⁴.

μιερός, μιεροφαγία, μιεροφαγεῖν, μιεροφονία all in Maccabees only.

τεσσεράκοντα Dt. 9⁹, ¹¹ : Josh. 14⁷.

SYNTAX

38. The Construction of the LXX not Greek. In treating of Accidence we have been concerned only with dialectical varieties within the Greek language, but in turning to syntax we come unavoidably upon what is not Greek. For the LXX is on the whole a literal translation, that is to say, it is only half a translation — the vocabulary has been changed, but seldom the construction. We have therefore to deal with a work of which the vocabulary is Greek and the syntax Hebrew.

39. Absence of μέν and δέ. How little we are concerned with a piece of Greek diction is brought home to us by the fact that the balance of clauses by the particles μέν and δέ, so familiar a feature of Greek style, is rare in the LXX, except in the books of Wisdom and Maccabees. It does not occur once in all the books between Deuteronomy and Proverbs nor in Ecclesiastes, the Song, the bulk of the Minor Prophets, Jeremiah, and Ezekiel; and in each of the following books it occurs once only — Leviticus (27⁷), Numbers (22³³), Tobit (14¹⁰), Haggai (1⁴), Zechariah (1¹⁵), Isaiah (6²). Where the antithesis is employed, it is often not managed with propriety, e.g. in Job 32⁶. As instances of the non-occurrence of one or both of the particles where their presence is obviously required we may take —

> Gen. 27²² Ἡ φωνὴ φωνὴ Ἰακώβ, αἱ δὲ χεῖρες χεῖρες Ἡσαύ. Jdg. 16²⁹ καὶ ἐκράτησεν ἕνα τῇ δεξίᾳ αὐτοῦ καὶ ἕνα τῇ ἀριστερᾷ αὐτοῦ. ii K. 11²⁵ ποτὲ μὲν οὕτως καὶ ποτὲ οὕτως. iii K. 18⁶ μιᾷ . . . ἄλλῃ.

40. Paratactical Construction of the LXX. Roughly speaking, it is true to say that in the Greek of the LXX there is no syntax, only parataxis. The whole is one great scheme of clauses connected by καί, and we have to trust to the sense to tell us which is to be so emphasized as to make it into the apodosis. It may therefore be laid down as a general rule that in the LXX the apodosis is introduced by καί. This is a recurrence to an earlier stage of language than that which Greek itself had reached long before the LXX was written, but we find occasional survivals of it in classical writers, e.g. Xen. *Cyrop.* I 4 § 28 καὶ ὁδόν τε οὔπω πολλὴν διηνύσθαι αὐτοῖς καὶ τὸν Μῆδον ἤκειν. Here it is convenient to translate καί 'when,' but the construction is really paratactical. So again Xen. *Anab.* IV 2 § 12 Καὶ τοῦτόν τε παρεληλύθεσαν οἱ Ἕλληνες, καὶ ἕτερον ὁρῶσιν ἔμπροσθεν λόφον κατεχόμενον. *Cp. Anab.* I 8 § 8, II 1 § 7, IV 6 § 2; also Verg. *Æn.* II 692 —

> Vix ea fatus erat senior, subitoque fragore
> intonuit laevom.

In the above instances the two clauses are coördinate. But in the LXX, even when the former clause is introduced by a subordinative conjunction, καί still follows in the latter, e.g. —

Gen. 44²⁹ ἐὰν οὖν λάβητε . . . καὶ κατάξετε κτλ.   Ex. 13¹⁴ ἐὰν δὲ ἐρωτήσῃ . . . καὶ ἐρεῖς κτλ.   *Cp.* 7⁹.   Josh. 4¹ καὶ ἐπεὶ συνετέλεσεν πᾶς ὁ λαὸς διαβαίνων τὸν Ἰορδάνην, καὶ εἶπεν Κύριος.

Sometimes a preposition with a verbal noun takes the place of the protasis, e.g. —

Ex. 3¹² ἐν τῷ ἐξαγαγεῖν . . . καὶ λατρεύσετε.

In Homer also καί is used in the apodosis after ἐπεί (*Od.* V 96), ἦμος (*Il.* I 477 : *Od.* X 188), or ὅτε (*Od.* V 391, 401 : X 145, 157, 250).

The difficulty which sometimes arises in the LXX in determining which is the apodosis amid a labyrinth of καὶ clauses, e.g. in Gen. 4¹⁴, 39¹⁰, may be paralleled by the difficulty which sometimes presents itself in Homer with regard to a series of clauses introduced by δέ, e.g. *Od.* X 112, 113; XI 34–6.

41. Introduction of the Sentence by a Verb of Being. Very often in imitation of Hebrew idiom the whole sentence is introduced by ἐγένετο or ἔσται.

Gen. 39¹⁹ ἐγένετο δὲ ὡς ἤκουσεν . . . καὶ ἐθυμώθη ὀργῇ. *Cp.* vs. 5, 7, 13.   iii K. 18¹² καὶ ἔσται ἐὰν ἐγὼ ἀπέλθω ἀπὸ σοῦ, καὶ πνεῦμα Κυρίου ἀρεῖ σε εἰς τὴν γῆν ἣν οὐκ οἶδας.

In such cases in accordance with western ideas of what a sentence ought to be, we say that καί introduces the apodosis, but it may be that, in its original conception at least, the whole construction was paratactical. It is easy to see this in a single instance like —

Gen. 41⁸ ἐγένετο δὲ πρωὶ καὶ ἐταράχθη ἡ ψυχὴ αὐτοῦ,

but the same explanation may be applied to more complex cases, *e.g.* —

Nb. 21⁹ καὶ ἐγένετο ὅταν ἔδακνεν ὄφις ἄνθρωπον, καὶ ἐπέβλεψεν ἐπὶ τὸν ὄφιν τὸν χαλκοῦν, καὶ ἔζη.   And *there was* when a serpent bit a man, and he looked on the brazen serpent, and lived.   *Cp.* Gen. 42³⁵, 43², ²¹: Jdg. 14¹¹.

42. Apposition of Verbs.   Sometimes the καί does not appear after ἐγένετο, ἐγενήθη, or ἔσται, thus presenting a construction which we may denote by the phrase Apposition of Verbs.

Jdg. 19³⁰ καὶ ἐγένετο πᾶς ὁ βλέπων ἔλεγεν . . .   i K. 31⁸ καὶ ἐγενήθη τῇ ἐπαύριον, ἔρχονται οἱ ἀλλόφυλοι.   Gen. 44³¹ καὶ ἔσται ἐν τῷ ἰδεῖν αὐτὸν μὴ ὂν τὸ παιδάριον μεθ᾽ ἡμῶν, τελευτήσει.

In two versions of the same Hebrew we find one translator using the καί and the other not.

iv K. 19¹ καὶ ἐγένετο ὡς ἤκουσεν βασιλεὺς Ἐζεκίας, καὶ διέρρηξεν τὰ ἱμάτια ἑαυτοῦ.   Is. 37¹ καὶ ἐγένετο ἐν τῷ ἀκοῦσαι τὸν βασιλέα Ἐζεκίαν, ἔσχισεν τὰ ἱμάτια.

43. Δέ in the Apodosis.   The use of δέ to mark the apodosis, which is found occasionally in classical authors from Homer downwards, is rare in the LXX.

Josh. 2⁸ καὶ ἐγένετο ὡς ἐξήλθοσαν . . . αὕτη δὲ ἀνέβη.

THE ARTICLE, 44, 45

44. Generic Use of the Article.   This is due to following the Hebrew.

i K. 17³⁴ ὁ λέων καὶ ἡ ἄρκος = 'a lion or a bear,' 17³⁶ καὶ τὴν ἄρκον ἔτυπτεν ὁ δοῦλός σου καὶ τὸν λέοντα.   Amos 5¹⁹ ὃν τρόπον ἐὰν φύγῃ ἄνθρωπος ἐκ προσώπου τοῦ λέοντος, καὶ ἐμπέσῃ αὐτῷ ἡ ἄρκος. Is. 7¹⁴ ἰδοὺ ἡ παρθένος ἐν γαστρὶ λήμψεται.

45. Elliptical Use of the Feminine Article.   The use of the feminine article with some case of χώρα or γῆ understood is not due to the influence of the Hebrew.

ἡ ὑπ᾽ οὐρανόν Job 18⁴.
τὴν ὑπ᾽ οὐρανόν Job 1⁷, 2², 5¹⁰, 9⁶, 28²⁴, 34¹³, 38²⁴.
τῆς ὑπὸ τὸν οὐρανόν Ex. 17⁴: Prov. 8²⁸: ii Mac. 2¹⁸.
τῆς ὑπ᾽ οὐρανόν Job 38¹⁸.
τῇ ὑπ᾽ οὐρανόν Esther 4¹⁷: Baruch 5³.

So in N.T. —

Lk. 17²⁴ ἡ ἀστραπὴ ἀστράπτουσα ἐκ τῆς ὑπὸ τὸν οὐρανὸν εἰς τὴν ὑπ' οὐρανόν λάμπει.

GENDER, 46, 47

46. Elliptical Use of the Feminine Adjective. There is nothing about the feminine gender which should make ellipse more frequent with it than with the masculine or neuter. Only it happens that some of the words which can be most easily supplied are feminine. This elliptical use of the feminine adjective (or of adv. = adj.) is a feature of Greek generally. It is not very common in the LXX. Instances are —

ἐπ' εὐθείας (ὁδοῦ) Josh. 8¹⁴.

ἐν τῇ εὐθείᾳ Ps. 142¹⁰.

τῆς πλατείας Esther 4¹.

τὴν σύμπασαν (γῆν) Job 2², 25².

ἔως τῆς σήμερον (ἡμέρας) ii Chr. 35²⁵.

τὴν αὔριον iii Mac. 5³⁸.

ἐβόησεν μεγάλῃ (τῇ φωνῇ) iv K. 18²⁸.

εἰς τὴν ὑψηλήν (χώραν) ii Chr. 1³.

In the N.T. this idiom occurs much more frequently. Take for instance Lk. 12⁴⁷, ⁴⁸ δαρήσεται πολλάς . . . ὀλίγας (πληγάς).

Cp. also —

τὴν πρὸς θάνατον (ὁδόν) Eus. H.E. II 23.

οὐκ εἰς μακράν Philo Leg. ad C. § 4.

ἐπ' εὐθείας Philo Q.O.P.L. § 1.

ἐπὶ ξένης (χώρας or γῆς) Philo Leg. ad C. § 3.

πεδιάς τε καὶ ὀρεινή ibid. § 7.

τῇ πατρίῳ (γλώσσῃ) Jos. B. J. Procem. 1.

τὰς περιοίκους (πόλεις) ibid. 8.

47. Feminine for Neuter. The use of the feminine for the neuter is a pure Hebraism, which occurs principally in the Psalms.

Jdg. 15⁷ ἐὰν ποιήσητε οὕτως ταύτην, 21³ εἰς τί . . . ἐγενήθη αὕτη; i K. 4⁷ οὐ γέγονεν τοιαύτη ἐχθὲς καὶ τρίτην. Ps. 26³ ἐν ταύτῃ ἐγὼ ἐλπίζω, 26⁴ μίαν ᾐτησάμην . . . ταύτην ἐκζητήσω, 31⁶ ὑπὲρ ταύτης προσεύξεται πᾶς ὅσιος, 117²³ παρὰ Κυρίου ἐγένετο αὕτη, 118⁵⁰ αὕτη με παρεκάλεσεν, 118⁵⁶ αὕτη ἐγενήθη μοι.

In the N.T. this license only occurs in Mk. 12¹¹, Mt. 21⁴² in a quotation from Ps. 117²³.

48. Singular for Plural. Sometimes in imitation of Hebrew idiom we find the singular used in the sense of the plural. When the article is employed along with a singular noun, we have the Generic Use of the Article (§ 44), but the presence of the article is not necessary.

Ex. 8⁶ ἀνεβιβάσθη ὁ βάτραχος (= frogs), 8¹⁸ ἐξαγαγεῖν τὸν σκνῖφα, 10¹³ καὶ ὁ ἄνεμος ὁ νότος ἀνέλαβεν τὴν ἀκρίδα, 10¹⁴ οὐ γέγονεν τοιαύτη ἀκρίς. Jdg. 7¹² ὡσεὶ ἀκρὶς εἰς πλῆθος (cp. Judith 2²⁰ ὡς ἀκρίς), 21¹⁶ ἠφανίσθη ἀπὸ Βενιαμεὶν γυνή. iv K. 2¹² ἅρμα Ἰσραὴλ καὶ ἱππεὺς αὐτοῦ. Ezk. 47⁹ ἔσται ἐκεῖ ἰχθὺς πολὺς σφόδρα.

This throws light on an otherwise startling piece of grammar — Jdg. 15¹⁰ εἶπαν ἀνὴρ Ἰούδα.

49. Singular Verb with more than One Subject. In accordance with Hebrew idiom a singular verb often introduces a plurality of subjects, e.g. —

iv K. 18²⁶ καὶ εἶπεν Ἐλιακεὶμ . . . καὶ Σόμνας καὶ Ἰώας, 18³⁷ καὶ εἰσῆλθεν Ἐλιακεὶμ κτλ.

This may happen also in Greek apart from Hebrew.

Xen. Anab. II 4 § 16 Ἔπεμψέ με Ἀριαῖος καὶ Ἀρτάοζος.

CASE, 50–61

50. Nominative for Vocative. a. The use of the nominative for the vocative was a colloquialism in classical Greek. It occurs in Plato, and is common in Aristophanes and Lucian. When so employed, the nominative usually has the article. As in Hebrew the vocative is regularly expressed by the nominative with the article, it is not surprising that the LXX translators should often avail themselves of this turn of speech.

iii K. 17¹⁸ τί ἐμοὶ καὶ σοί, ὁ ἄνθρωπος τοῦ Θεοῦ; 18²⁶ ἐπάκουσον ἡμῶν, ὁ Βάαλ. Cp. iii K. 20²⁰: Ps. 21¹, 42².

For an instance of the nominative without the article standing for the vocative take —

Baruch 4⁵ θαρσεῖτε, λαός μου.

The nominative, when thus employed, is often put in apposition with a vocative, as —

iii K. 17²⁰ Κύριε, ὁ μάρτυς τῆς χήρας, 17²¹ Κύριε, ὁ Θεός μου.

b. In the N.T. also the nominative with the article is often put for the vocative.

Mt. 11²⁶ ναί, ὁ πατήρ.   Lk. 8⁵⁴ ἡ παῖς, ἐγείρου.   Mk. 9²⁵ τὸ πνεῦμα τὸ ἄλαλον . . . ἔξελθε.   Lk. 6²⁵ οὐαὶ ὑμῖν, οἱ ἐμπεπλησμένοι νῦν. Col. 3¹⁸ αἱ γυναῖκες, ὑποτάσσεσθε.   Eph. 6¹, Col. 3²⁰ τὰ τέκνα, ὑπακούετε.

The use of the nominative without the article for the vocative is rare in the N.T., as it is also in the LXX. In Lk. 12²⁰ and i Cor. 15³⁶ we find ἄφρων put for ἄφρον, and in Acts 7⁴² οἶκος Ἰσραήλ does duty as vocative.

As instances of apposition of nominative with vocative we may take—

Rom. 2¹ ὦ ἄνθρωπε πᾶς ὁ κρίνων.   Rev. 15³ Κύριε ὁ Θεός, ὁ παντοκράτωρ.

In Rev. 18²⁰ we have vocative and nominative conjoined—

οὐρανέ, καὶ οἱ ἅγιοι.

51. Nominative Absolute. Occasionally we get a construction in the LXX, which can be described only by this name.

Nb. 22²⁴ καὶ ἔστη ὁ ἄγγελος τοῦ θεοῦ ἐν ταῖς αὔλαξιν τῶν ἀμπέλων, φραγμὸς ἐντεῦθεν καὶ φραγμὸς ἐντεῦθεν.   Nb. 24⁴ ὅστις ὅρασιν θεοῦ εἶδεν, ἐν ὕπνῳ, ἀποκεκαλυμμένοι οἱ ὀφθαλμοὶ αὐτοῦ.

As this construction arises out of a literal following of the Hebrew, it would be superfluous to adduce Greek parallels. Like effects might be found, but the cause would be different.

52. Nominative of Reference. What is meant by this term will be best understood from the examples—

Job 28⁷ τρίβος, οὐκ ἔγνω αὐτὴν πετεινόν.   Ps. 102¹⁵ ἄνθρωπος, ὡσεὶ χόρτος αἱ ἡμέραι αὐτοῦ.

To throw out the subject of discourse first, and then proceed to speak about it, is a Hebraism, but at the same time it is a common resource of language generally.

So in N.T.—

Acts 7⁴⁰ ὁ γὰρ Μωσῆς οὗτος . . . οὐκ οἴδαμεν τί ἐγένετο αὐτῷ.   Rev. 3¹² ὁ νικῶν, ποιήσω αὐτὸν στῦλον ἐν τῷ ναῷ τοῦ Θεοῦ μου.

53. Nominativus Pendens. The nominative which is left without a verb owing to a sudden change of construction is a familiar feature in classical Greek, especially if this be at all colloquial. It is not however very common in the LXX.

Dan. O' 7¹⁵ καὶ ἀκηδιάσας ἐγὼ . . . ἐτάρασσόν με.

Such cases can generally be explained on the principle of construction according to the sense.

It is seldom that we meet with so violent an anacoluthon as the following in the N.T. —

Mk. 9²⁰ καὶ ἰδὼν αὐτόν, τὸ πνεῦμα εὐθὺς συνεσπάραξεν αὐτόν.

54. Accusative for Vocative. The accusative for vocative might seem an impossibility, yet here is an instance of it.

Ps. 51⁶ ἠγάπησας πάντα τὰ ῥήματα καταποντίσμου, γλῶσσαν δολίαν.

55. Accusative of Time When. In connexion with classical Greek we think of Time When as being expressed by the genitive or dative, rather than by the accusative, though the latter also is used. The employment of the accusative became more frequent after the classical period, and alone survives in the modern language.

Gen. 43¹⁶ μετ' ἐμοῦ γὰρ φάγονται οἱ ἄνθρωποι ἄρτους τὴν μεσημβρίαν.

Ex. 9¹⁸ ἰδοὺ ἐγὼ ὕω ταύτην τὴν ὥραν αὔριον χάλαζαν.

Dan. Θ 9²¹ ὡσεὶ ὥραν θυσίας ἑσπερινῆς (O' has ἐν ὥρᾳ).

So also sometimes in N.T.—

Jn. 4⁵² χθὲς ὥραν ἑβδόμην ἀφῆκεν αὐτὸν ὁ πυρετός. Rev. 3³ καὶ οὐ μὴ γνῷς ποίαν ὥραν ἥξω ἐπί σε.

56. Cognate Accusative. *a.* By a Cognate Accusative is here meant that particular form of the *Figura Etymologica* in which a verb is followed by an accusative of kindred derivation with itself, irrespective of the question whether it be an accusative of the external or of the internal object. We have both kinds of accusative together in the following verse, where θήραν = venison.

Gen. 27³ ἐξέστη δὲ Ἰσαὰκ ἔκστασιν μεγάλην σφόδρα καὶ εἶπεν "Τίς οὖν ὁ θηρεύσας μοι θήραν;"

b. The great frequency of the cognate accusative in the LXX is due to the fact that here the genius of the Hebrew and of the Greek language coincides. Besides being a legitimate Greek usage, this construction is also one of the means employed for translating a constantly recurring Hebrew formula. Sometimes the appended accusative merely supplies an object to the verb, as in such phrases

as δάνιον δανείζειν, διαθέσθαι διαθήκην, διηγεῖσθαι διήγημα, ἐνύπνιον ἐνυπνιά-
ζεσθαι, ἐπιθυμεῖν ἐπιθυμίαν, θύειν θυσίαν, νηστεύειν νηστείαν, ὁρισμὸν ὁρίζε-
σθαι, πλημμελεῖν πλημμέλησιν or πλημμελίαν, προφασίζεσθαι προφάσεις.
At other times it is accompanied by some specification, as —

    Nb. 18⁶ λειτουργεῖν τὰς λειτουργίας τῆς σκηνῆς τοῦ μαρτυρίου.   Dan.
11² πλουτήσει πλοῦτον μέγαν.   i Mac. 2⁵⁸ ἐν τῷ ζηλῶσαι ζῆλον
νόμου.

c. Sometimes the cognate accusative is conveyed in a relative
clause, as —

    Ex. 3⁹ τὸν θλιμμὸν ὃν οἱ Αἰγύπτιοι θλίβουσιν αὐτούς.   Nb. 1⁴⁴ ἡ
ἐπίσκεψις ἣν ἐπεσκέψαντο.   i K. 2²³ ἡ ἀκοὴ ἣν ἐγὼ ἀκούω.

d. By other changes of construction we have still the *figura etymologica*, but no longer a cognate accusative. Thus, starting from
the common phrase δοῦναι δόμα, we have δεδομένοι δόμα (Nb. 3⁹) and
δόμα δεδομένον (Nb. 18⁶).

    e. In one instance the cognate accusative is reinforced by a still
further application of the etymological figure —

    Gen. 47²² ἐν δόσει γὰρ ἔδωκεν δόμα τοῖς ἱερεῦσιν.

This is not due to the Hebrew.

    f. In a wider sense the term 'cognate accusative' includes an
accusative of kindred meaning, though not of kindred derivation,
as —

    Jdg. 15⁸ ἐπάταξεν . . . πληγὴν μεγάλην.

    g. Instances of cognate accusative are common enough in the N.T.,
e.g. —

    i Jn. 5¹⁶ ἁμαρτάνοντα ἁμαρτίαν μὴ πρὸς θάνατον.   Mt. 2¹⁰ ἐχάρησαν
χαρὰν μεγάλην σφόδρα.   Jn. 7²⁴ τὴν δικαίαν κρίσιν κρίνατε.

There also it occurs sometimes in a relative clause —

    Mk. 10³⁸ τὸ βάπτισμα ὃ ἐγὼ βαπτίζομαι.   Jn. 17²⁶ ἡ ἀγάπη ἣν ἠγά-
πηκάς με.   Eph. 4¹ τῆς κλήσεως ἧς ἐκλήθητε.

    h. We have a triple use of the etymological figure in —

    Lk. 8⁵ ἐξῆλθεν ὁ σπείρων τοῦ σπεῖραι τὸν σπόρον αὐτοῦ.

    i. That the playing with paronymous terms is in accordance with
the spirit of the Greek language may be seen from the frequent
employment of the device by Plato, *e.g.* —

    Prot. 326 D ὥσπερ οἱ γραμματισταὶ τοῖς μήπω δεινοῖς γράφειν τῶν
παίδων ὑπογράψαντες γραμμὰς τῇ γραφίδι οὕτω τὸ γραμματεῖον δι-

δόασι. *Hip. Maj.* 296 C Ἄλλα μέντοι δυνάμει γε δύνανται οἱ
δυνάμενοι· οὐ γάρ που ἀδυναμίᾳ γε.

57. Accusative in Apposition to Indeclinable Noun. In the LXX an
indeclinable noun is sometimes followed by an accusative in apposition to it, even though by the rules of grammar it is itself in some
other case, *e.g.* —

Is. 37³⁸ ἐν τῷ οἴκῳ Νασαρὰχ τὸν πάτραρχον αὐτοῦ. iv K. 1² ἐν τῷ
Βάαλ μυῖαν θεὸν Ἀκκαρών.

Perhaps it would be more satisfactory if this and § 54 were thrown
together under a head of Bad Grammar, a category which the reader
might be inclined to enlarge.

58. Genitive Absolute. Strictly speaking, a Genitive Absolute is
a clause in the genitive which does not affect the general construction. It ought not therefore to refer either to the subject or the
object of the sentence. Even in classical authors however the so-
called genitive absolute is sometimes not employed with the pre-
cision which grammarians might desire, *e.g.* —

Plat. *Rep.* 547 B βιαζομένων δὲ καὶ ἀντιτεινόντων ἀλλήλοις . . . ὡμο-
λόγησαν.   Xen. *Cyrop.* I 4 § 2 καὶ γὰρ ἀσθενήσαντος αὐτοῦ οὐδέποτε ἀπέλειπε τὸν πάππον.   Xen. *Anab.* I 2 § 17 θᾶσσον προϊόν-
των . . . δρόμος ἐγένετο τοῖς στρατιώταις.

The genitive absolute is often employed in the same loose way
in the LXX.

Tob. 4¹ ὅτε ἤμην ἐν τῇ χώρᾳ μου . . . νεωτέρου μου ὄντος.
Dt. 15¹⁰ οὐ λυπηθήσῃ τῇ καρδίᾳ σου διδόντος σου αὐτῷ.
Ex. 2¹⁰ ἀδρυνθέντος δὲ τοῦ παιδίου, εἰσήγαγεν αὐτό.
Ex. 5²⁰ συνήντησαν δὲ . . . ἐρχομένοις . . . ἐκπορευομένων αὐτῶν.

So in N.T. —

Mt. 1¹⁸ μνηστευθείσης τῆς μητρὸς . . . εὑρέθη.   Acts 21¹⁷ γενομέ-
νων δὲ ἡμῶν εἰς Ἱεροσόλυμα ἀσμένως ἀπεδέξαντο ἡμᾶς οἱ ἀδελφοί.
ii Cor. 4¹⁸ κατεργάζεται ἡμῖν, μὴ σκοπούντων ἡμῶν.

59. The Genitive Infinitive of Purpose. The genitive of the verbal
noun formed by prefixing the article to the infinitive, which we may
call for convenience the Genitive Infinitive, is one of the regular
ways of expressing purpose in Biblical Greek, corresponding to our
use of 'to.' The construction is not entirely unknown to classical
authors (*e.g.* Plat. *Gorg.* 457 E τοῦ καταφανὲς γενέσθαι) and is especially

favoured by Thucydides. There is nothing in the Hebrew to suggest it. The following will serve as examples —

Jdg. 16⁵ καὶ δήσομεν αὐτὸν τοῦ ταπεινῶσαι αὐτόν.   Ps. 9³⁰ ἐνεδρεύει τοῦ ἁρπάσαι πτωχόν.   Job 1¹⁹ ἦλθον τοῦ ἀπαγγεῖλαί σοι.

So also frequently in N.T., e.g. —

Mt. 13³ ἐξῆλθεν ὁ σπείρων τοῦ σπείρειν.   James 5¹⁷ προσηύξατο τοῦ μὴ βρέξαι.

60. Other Uses of the Genitive Infinitive. a. The genitive infinitive of purpose is only one use out of many to which this syntactical device is applied. Take for instance —

Ex. 14⁵ Τί τοῦτο ἐποιήσαμεν τοῦ ἐξαποστεῖλαι τοὺς υἱοὺς Ἰσραὴλ τοῦ μὴ δουλεύειν ἡμῖν (= ὥστε μὴ δουλεύειν);

Purpose is not expressed in either of these cases. In the former we have what may be called the Explanatory Use of the Genitive Infinitive; in the latter we have something which represents 'from serving us' in the original, but which we shall nevertheless class as a Genitive Infinitive of Consequence, since it is only thus that the Greek can be explained.

b. The Explanatory Use of the Genitive Infinitive is common in the LXX, e.g. —

Gen. 3²² Ἰδοὺ Ἀδὰμ γέγονεν ὡς εἷς ἐξ ἡμῶν, τοῦ γιγνώσκειν καλὸν καὶ πονηρόν.   Ex. 8²⁹ μὴ προσθῇς ἔτι, Φαραώ, ἐξαπατῆσαι τοῦ μὴ ἐξαποστεῖλαι τὸν λαόν.   Ps. 26⁴ ταύτην (§ 47) ἐκζητήσω· τοῦ κατοικεῖν με κτλ.

So in N.T. —

Acts 7¹⁹ ἐκάκωσε τοὺς πατέρας ἡμῶν, τοῦ ποιεῖν ἔκθετα τὰ βρέφη αὐτῶν. Gal. 3¹⁰ ὃς οὐκ ἐμμένει ἐν πᾶσι τοῖς γεγραμμένοις . . . τοῦ ποιῆσαι αὐτά.

c. As an instance of the Genitive Infinitive of Consequence we may take —

Ex. 7¹⁴ βεβάρηται ἡ καρδία Φαραὼ τοῦ μὴ ἐξαποστεῖλαι τὸν λαόν.

So in N.T. —

Hb. 11⁵ Ἐνὼχ μετετέθη τοῦ μὴ ἰδεῖν θάνατον.

d. What is called in Latin Grammar the 'prolative infinitive' after 'extensible' verbs, or more simply, the latter of two verbs, is also commonly expressed in the LXX by the genitive infinitive, e.g. —

Ps. 39¹³ οὐκ ἠδυνάσθην τοῦ βλέπειν.   ii Chr. 3¹ ἤρξατο τοῦ οἰκοδομεῖν.   Gen. 18⁷ ἐτάχυνεν τοῦ ποιῆσαι αὐτό.

So in N.T. —

Acts 3¹² ὡς . . . πεποιηκόσι τοῦ περιπατεῖν αὐτόν, 15²⁰ ἐπιστεῖλαι . . .
τοῦ ἀπέχεσθαι, 27¹ ἐκρίθη τοῦ ἀποπλεῖν.

61. Cognate Dative. a. Another form of the *figura etymologica*
which abounds in the LXX may be called Cognate Dative. As in
the case of the cognate accusative its frequency is in great measure
due to the coincidence of idiom in this particular between Greek
and Hebrew. Let us first show by a few examples from Plato that
this construction is in accordance with the genius of the Greek
language.

Crat. 385 B λόγῳ λέγειν. Phdr. 265 C παιδίᾳ πεπαῖσθαι. Symp.
195 B φεύγων φυγῇ τὸ γῆρας. Crat. 383 A φύσει . . . πεφυκυῖαν.
Cp. 389 C, D. Phileb. 14 C φύσει . . . πεφυκότα.

b. But while we have to search for this idiom in classical Greek,
it thrusts itself upon us at every turn in the Greek of the LXX,
owing to its aptness for rendering a mode of expression familiar in
the original.

c. Corresponding to the cognate dative in Greek, we find in Latin
also a cognate ablative as a rare phenomenon, e.g. —

   curriculo percurre Ter. *Heaut.* 733. Cp. Plaut. *Most.* 349
     qui non curro curriculo domum.
   occidione occisum Cic. *Fam.* XV 4 § 7. Cp. Liv. II 51 § 9.

d. The instances of cognate dative of most frequent occurrence in
the LXX are ἀκοῇ ἀκούειν, ζωῇ ζῆν, θανάτῳ ἀποθανεῖν, θανάτῳ θανατοῦσθαι,
σάλπιγγι σαλπίζειν. But besides these there are many others, as —

ἀγαπήσει ἀγαπᾶσθαι	ἐκλείψει ἐκλείπειν
ἀλαλαγμῷ ἀλαλάζειν	ἐκτριβῇ ἐκτριβῆναι
ἀλοιφῇ ἐξαλείφειν	ἐκτρίψει ἐκτριβῆναι
ἀπωλίᾳ ἀπολλύναι	ἐξερανᾶν ἐξεραυνήσει
ἀφανισμῷ ἀφανίζειν	ἐξουδενώσει ἐξουδενοῦν
βδελύγματι βδελύσσειν	ἐπιθυμίᾳ ἐπιθυμεῖν
δεσμῷ δεῖν	ἐπισκοπῇ ἐπισκέπτεσθαι
διαλύσει διαλύειν	θελήσει θέλειν
διαμαρτυρίᾳ διαμαρτυρεῖν	καθαιρέσει καθαίρειν
διαφθείρειν φθορᾷ	καθαρισμῷ καθαρίζειν
δίκῃ ἐκδικεῖν	κακίᾳ κακοποιεῖν
ἐκβάλλειν ἐκβολῇ	κακίᾳ κακοῦν
ἐκθλίβειν ἐκθλιβῇ	κατάραις καταρᾶσθαι

κλαυθμῷ κλαίειν	πλημμελίᾳ πλημμελεῖν
λήθῃ λαθεῖν	προνομῇ προνομευθῆναι
λίθοις λιθοβολεῖν	προσοχθίσματι προσοχθίζειν
λύτροις λυτροῦν	πτώσει πίπτειν
μνείᾳ μνησθῆναι	ταλαιπωρίᾳ ταλαιπωρεῖν
οἰωνισμῷ οἰωνίζεσθαι	ταραχῇ ταράσσειν
ὀργίζεσθαι ὀργῇ	ὑπεροράσει ὑπεριδεῖν
ὅρκῳ ὁρκίζειν	φερνῇ φερνίζειν
παραδόσει παραδοθῆναι	φθορᾷ φθαρῆναι
περιπίπτειν περιπτώματι	χαίρειν χαρᾷ

e. From the foregoing instances it is an easy step to others in which the substantive is of kindred meaning, though not of kindred derivation with the verb.

Gen. 1^{16} βρώσει φάγῃ, 31^{15} κατέφαγεν καταβρώσει. Ex. 19^{12}, $21^{16, 17}$ θανάτῳ τελευτᾶν. Ex. 22^{20} θανάτῳ ὀλεθρευθήσεται. Nb. 11^{15} ἀπόκτεινόν με ἀναίρεσει, 35^{26} ἐξόδῳ ἐξέλθῃ. Ezk. 33^{27} θανάτῳ ἀποκτενῶ.

f. Instances of the cognate dative are to be found also in the N.T., though not with anything like the frequency with which they occur in the LXX.

Jn. 3^{29} χαρᾷ χαίρει. Lk. 22^{15} ἐπιθυμίᾳ ἐπεθύμησα. Acts 4^{17} ἀπειλῇ (margin) ἀπειλησώμεθα, 5^{28} παραγγελίᾳ παρηγγείλαμεν, 23^{14} ἀναθέματι ἀναθεματίσαμεν. James 5^{17} προσευχῇ προσηύξατο. Gal. 5^1 τῇ ἐλευθερίᾳ ἡμᾶς Χριστὸς ἠλευθέρωσε.

g. The expression in ii Pet. 3^3 ἐν ἐμπαιγμονῇ ἐμπαῖκται, while not exactly parallel with the foregoing, belongs to the same range of idiom; so also Rev. 2^{23} ἀποκτενῶ ἐν θανάτῳ.

ADJECTIVES, 62–65

62. ἥμισυς. In Attic Greek ἥμισυς, like some other adjectives, mostly of quantity, has a peculiar construction. It governs a noun in the genitive, but agrees with it in gender. Thus —

Plat. *Phœdo* 104 A ὁ ἥμισυς τοῦ ἀριθμοῦ ἅπας. Thuc. V 31 § 2 ἐπὶ τῇ ἡμισείᾳ τῆς γῆς. Demosth. p. 44, iv 16 τοῖς ἡμίσεσι τῶν ἱππέων.

This idiom is kept up by Hellenistic writers, such as Philo, Strabo, and the translator of Josephus' *Jewish War*. It is however very rare in the LXX, occurring only in the following passages —

iii K. 16⁹ ὁ ἄρχων τῆς ἡμίσους (§ 11) τῆς ἵππου.   Josh. 4¹², i Chr. 5²³ οἱ ἡμίσεις φυλῆς Μανασσή.   Tob. 10¹⁰ τὰ ἥμισυ (sic) τῶν ὑπαρχόντων.   Ezk. 16⁵¹ τὰς ἡμίσεις τῶν ἁμαρτιῶν.   i Mac. 3³⁴, ³⁷ τὰς ἡμίσεις τῶν δυνάμεων.

Elsewhere instead of the Attic idiom we find τὸ ἥμισυ or ἥμισυ, irrespective of the gender and number of the noun which follows, e.g. —

τὸ ἥμισυ τοῦ σίκλου Ex. 39².	ἥμισυ ἀρχόντων ii Esd. 4¹⁶.
τὸ ἥμισυ αὐτῆς Lvt. 6²⁰.	ἐν ἡμίσει ἡμερῶν Ps. 101²⁵.
τὸ ἥμισυ τοῦ αἵματος Ex. 24⁶.	τὸ ἥμισυ τῶν ὑπαρχόντων Tob. 8²¹.

63. πᾶς.   *a.* In classical Greek the rule for πᾶς in the singular is that with the article it is collective, without the article it is distributive —

πᾶσα ἡ πόλις = all the city.
πᾶσα πόλις   = every city.

πᾶς differs from ordinary adjectives in taking the predicative position in an attributive sense.   Thus while ἀγαθὴ ἡ πόλις means 'the city is good,' πᾶσα ἡ πόλις means 'all the city.'   πᾶς may however also take the attributive position, like any other adjective.   When it does so, the collective force is intensified —

πᾶσα ἡ πόλις = all the city.
ἡ πᾶσα πόλις = the whole city.

Thus Plato's expression (*Apol.* 40 E) ὁ πᾶς χρόνος is rendered by Cicero (*T.D.* I § 97) perpetuitas omnis consequentis temporis.   For other instances of this use in classical authors we may take —

Hdt. VII 46 ὁ πᾶς ἀνθρώπινος βίος.   Plat. *Rep.* 618 B ὁ πᾶς κίνδυνος, *Phileb.* 67 B οἱ πάντες βόες = all the oxen in the world. Xen. *Anab.* V 6 § 5 οἱ πάντες ἄνθρωποι.

In such cases there is an additional stress gained by the unusual position assigned to πᾶς.

b. In the LXX the same distinction seems to be maintained.   It is true a writer will go from one to the other, e.g. —

Jdg. 16¹⁷, ¹⁸ καὶ ἀνήγγειλαν αὐτῇ τὴν πᾶσαν καρδίαν αὐτοῦ . . . καὶ εἶδεν Δαλειδὰ ὅτι ἀπήγγειλεν αὐτῇ πᾶσαν τὴν καρδίαν αὐτοῦ —

but so in English we might first say *he told her his whole heart,* and then add *and she saw that he had told her all his heart.*

Other instances of the strongly collective force of πᾶς in the attributive position are —

Gen. 45²⁰ τὰ γὰρ πάντα ἀγαθὰ Αἰγύπτου ὑμῖν ἔσται. Josh. 4¹⁴ ἐναντίον τοῦ παντὸς γένους Ἰσραήλ. Wisd. 7⁹ ὁ πᾶς χρυσός. ii Mac. 8⁹ τὸ πᾶν τῆς Ἰουδαίας . . . γένος.

Still there is a tendency in the LXX to assimilate πᾶς to adjectives generally and to employ it in the attributive position without any special emphasis.

c. Neither is the rule that πᾶς without the article is distributive at all closely adhered to, *e.g.* —

Ex. 8¹⁶ ἐν πάσῃ γῇ Αἰγύπτου, 16⁶ πρὸς πᾶσαν συναγωγὴν υἱῶν Ἰσραήλ. i K. 7² πᾶς οἶκος Ἰσραήλ.

d. In the plural οἱ πάντες is rare, but may be found —

Jdg. 20⁴⁶ οἱ πάντες οὗτοι. i Mac. 2³⁷ Ἀποθάνωμεν οἱ πάντες ἐν τῇ ἁπλότητι ἡμῶν. ii Mac. 12⁴⁰ τοῖς δὲ πᾶσι σαφὲς ἐγένετο. *Cp.* Aristeas § 36 τοῖς πᾶσι . . . πολίταις.

Αἱ πᾶσαι is still rarer, but see —

iii Mac. 1¹ παραγγείλας ταῖς πάσαις δυνάμεσιν.

Τὰ πάντα is comparatively common, occurring, *e.g.,* in Gen. 1³¹, 9³: Ex. 29²⁴: Lvt. 19¹³: ii Mac. 10²³, 12²²: iii Mac. 2³.

e. In the N.T. the collective use of πᾶς followed by the article is clearly marked in many passages, *e.g.* —

Gal. 5¹⁴ ὁ . . . πᾶς νόμος. Mt. 8³⁴ πᾶσα ἡ πόλις ἐξῆλθεν.

Also the distributive use of πᾶς without the article, as in i Cor. 11⁴,⁵ πᾶς ἀνήρ . . . πᾶσα δὲ γυνή. In Rom. 3¹⁹ we have the two usages brought into contrast — ἵνα πᾶν στόμα φραγῇ, καὶ ὑπόδικος γένηται πᾶς ὁ κόσμος τῷ Θεῷ.

On the other hand there are also instances of πᾶς in the singular and without the article being used collectively, *e.g.* —

Eph. 2²¹ πᾶσα οἰκοδομή. Mt. 2³ πᾶσα Ἱεροσόλυμα. Acts 2³⁶ πᾶς οἶκος Ἰσραήλ.

f. In the plural οἱ πάντες is more common in St. Paul than in the LXX. Take for instance —

Phil. 2²¹ οἱ πάντες γὰρ τὰ ἑαυτῶν ζητοῦσι. *Cp.* ii Cor. 5¹⁴. i Cor. 10¹⁷ οἱ γὰρ πάντες ἐκ τοῦ ἑνὸς ἄρτου μετέχομεν. *Cp.* Eph. 4¹³.

Rom. 11³² συνέκλεισε γὰρ ὁ Θεὸς τοὺς πάντας εἰς ἀπείθειαν.   ii Cor.
5¹⁰ τοὺς γὰρ πάντας ἡμᾶς κτλ.   i Cor. 9²² τοῖς πᾶσι γέγονα πάντα.

In Acts 19⁷ we have οἱ πάντες ἄνδρες.

Τὰ πάντα occurs in Rom. 8³², 11³⁶ : i Cor. 15²⁷, 12⁶, ¹⁹ : Eph. 5¹³ : Acts
17²⁵ : Mk. 4¹¹ and perhaps in other passages.

64. Comparison of Adjectives. Owing to the peculiarity of Hebrew
syntax the treatment of this subject mostly falls under the head of
Prepositions. We need only notice here that the positive may be
put for the comparative, and μᾶλλον omitted at will or inserted even
after a comparative.

Gen. 49¹² λευκοὶ οἱ ὀδόντες αὐτοῦ ἢ γάλα.   Dt. 7¹⁷ πολὺ τὸ ἔθνος
τοῦτο ἢ ἐγώ, 9¹ ἔθνη μεγάλα καὶ ἰσχυρότερα μᾶλλον ἢ ὑμεῖς.

So in N.T. —

Mt. 18⁸, ⁹ καλόν σοι ἐστὶν εἰσελθεῖν . . . ἢ . . . βληθῆναι.   Cp.
Mk. 9⁴³, ⁴⁵.

65. Omission of μᾶλλον. The comparison of attributes may be
effected by the use of verbs as well as of adjectives. In such cases
the omission of μᾶλλον is common in the LXX.

Nb. 22⁶ ἰσχύει οὗτος ἢ ἡμεῖς, 24⁷ ὑψωθήσεται ἢ Γὼγ βασιλεία.   Hos.
7⁶ ἔλεος θέλω ἢ θυσίαν.   ii Mac. 7² ἕτοιμοι γὰρ ἀποθνήσκειν
ἐσμὲν ἢ πατρῴους νόμους παραβαίνειν.

Cp. Aristeas § 322 τέρπειν γὰρ οἴομαί σε ταῦτα ἢ τὰ τῶν μυθολόγων βιβλία.

PRONOUNS, 66-71

66. Superfluous Use of Pronoun. A pronoun is sometimes employed
superfluously after the object, direct or indirect, has been already
expressed, e.g. —

Ex. 12⁴⁴ καὶ πᾶν (sic) οἰκέτην ἢ ἀργυρώνητον περιτεμεῖς αὐτόν.
Nb. 26³⁷ καὶ τῷ Σαλπαὰδ υἱῷ Ὀφερ οὐκ ἐγένοντο αὐτῷ υἱοί.

The above may be considered as deflexions of the Nominative of
Reference (§ 52) into an oblique case by Attraction.
So in N.T. —

ii Cor. 12¹⁷ μή τινα ὧν ἀπέσταλκα πρὸς ὑμᾶς, δι᾽ αὐτοῦ ἐπλεονέκτησα
ὑμᾶς ;   Mt. 25²⁹ τοῦ δὲ μὴ ἔχοντος, καὶ ὃ ἔχει ἀρθήσεται ἀπ᾽ αὐτοῦ.
Rev. 2⁷, ¹⁷ τῷ νικῶντι δώσω αὐτῷ.   Cp. 6⁴.

In Josh. 24²² — ὑμεῖς ἐξελέξασθε Κυρίῳ λατρεύειν αὐτῷ — Κυρίῳ should be τὸν Κύριον (which A has). Then λατρεύειν αὐτῷ would be an explanatory clause added after the usual manner.

67. Frequent Use of Pronouns. Apart from any Semitic influence there is also a tendency in later Greek to a much more lavish use of pronouns than was thought necessary by classical authors. We have seen already (§ 13) that the missing pronoun of the 3d person was supplied. The possessive use of the article moreover was no longer thought sufficient, and a possessive genitive was added, e.g. —

Gen. 38²⁷ καὶ τῇδε ἦν δίδυμα ἐν τῇ κοιλίᾳ αὐτῆς.

So in N.T. —

Mt. 19⁹ ὃς ἂν ἀπολύσῃ τὴν γυναῖκα αὐτοῦ.   i Pet. 2²⁴ αὐτὸς ἀνήνεγκεν ἐν τῷ σώματι αὐτοῦ.

68. Ἀδελφός as a Reciprocal Pronoun. The use of ἀδελφός as a reciprocal pronoun is a sheer Hebraism, e.g. —

Ex. 10²³ καὶ οὐκ εἶδεν οὐδεὶς τὸν ἀδελφὸν αὐτοῦ = they saw not one another.

69. Hebrew Syntax of the Relative. a. One of the most salient characteristics of LXX Greek is the repetition of the pronoun after the relative, as though in English, instead of saying 'the land which they possessed,' we were to say habitually 'the land which they possessed it,' and so in all similar cases. This anomaly is due to the literal following of the Hebrew text. Now in Hebrew the relative is indeclinable. Its meaning therefore is not complete until a pronoun has been added to determine it. But the relative in Greek being declinable, the translator was forced to assign to it gender, number, and case, which rendered the addition of the pronoun after it unnecessary. Nevertheless the pronoun was retained out of regard for the sacred text. As instances of the simplest kind we may take the following —

Nb. 35²⁵ ὃν ἔχρισαν αὐτόν, 13³³ τῆς γῆς ἣν κατεσκέψαντο αὐτήν.   Is. 62² ὃ ὁ κύριος ὀνομάσει αὐτό.   Gen. 1¹¹ οὗ τὸ σπέρμα αὐτοῦ ἐν αὐτῷ.   Dt. 4⁷ ᾧ ἐστιν αὐτῷ.   Ps. 18⁴ ὧν οὐχὶ ἀκούονται αἱ φωναὶ αὐτῶν.   Ex. 6²⁶ οἷς εἶπεν αὐτοῖς.

b. Where the relative is followed by ἐάν the same construction is employed, e.g. —

Nb. 17⁵ ὁ ἄνθρωπος ὃν ἐὰν ἐκλέξωμαι αὐτόν, 19²² παντὸς οὗ ἐὰν ἅψηται αὐτοῦ ὁ ἀκάθαρτος.

c. Sometimes a demonstrative takes the place of the personal pronoun —

Gen. 3¹¹ οὗ ἐνετειλάμην σοι τούτου μόνου μὴ φαγεῖν.

d. In all the foregoing instances the appended pronoun is in the same case as the relative, but this is not necessary.

Nb. 3³ οὓς ἐτελείωσεν τὰς χεῖρας αὐτῶν ἱερατεύειν.

The construction here, though determined by the Hebrew, happens to agree with the Greek Accusative of the Part Affected.

e. Very often there is the same preposition both before the relative and before the appended pronoun —

Ex. 34¹² εἰς ἣν εἰσπορεύῃ εἰς αὐτήν.   Nb. 11²¹ ἐν οἷς εἰμι ἐν αὐτοῖς.
Gen. 28¹³ ἡ γῆ ἐφ' ἧς σὺ καθεύδεις ἐπ' αὐτῆς.

f. Occasionally the preposition is the same, but the case it governs is different, *e.g.* —

Jdg. 16²⁶ ἐφ' οἷς ὁ οἶκος στήκει ἐπ' αὐτούς.   Josh. 24¹³ γῆν ἐφ' ἣν οὐκ ἐκοπιάσατε ἐπ' αὐτῆς.

g. Sometimes the preposition is confined to the appended pronoun. Then the problem arises, Into what case is the relative to be put? — a problem which is solved differently in different passages. In some the case chosen coincides with that of the pronoun following, *e.g.* —

Gen. 24⁴² τὴν ὁδόν μου, ἣν νῦν ἐγὼ πορεύομαι ἐπ' αὐτήν.   Ex. 25²⁸ τοὺς κυάθους, οἷς σπείσεις ἐν αὐτοῖς.   Gen. 21²³ τῇ γῇ ᾗ σὺ παρῴκησας ἐν αὐτῇ.

In others it does not —

Nb. 14³¹ τὴν γῆν ἣν ὑμεῖς ἀπέστητε ἀπ' αὐτῆς, 19² ᾗ οὐκ ἐπεβλήθη ἐπ' αὐτὴν ζυγός.   iii K. 17¹ ᾧ παρέστην ἐνώπιον αὐτοῦ.

h. Sometimes the relative has a different preposition from the pronoun following —

Nb. 13²⁰ τίς ἡ γῆ εἰς ἣν οὗτοι ἐνκάθηνται ἐπ' αὐτῆς . . . τίνες αἱ πόλεις εἰς ἃς οὗτοι κατοικοῦσιν ἐν αὐταῖς.   For other instances see Ex. 6⁴: Nb. 15³⁹: Dt. 1²², 1³³, 28⁴⁹.

i. Sometimes the preposition is the same, but instead of a mere pronoun we have a phrase, *e.g.* —

Gen. 24³⁸ ἐν οἷς ἐγὼ παροικῶ ἐν τῇ γῇ αὐτῶν.

j. The construction of which we have been speaking is not confined to the simple relative, *e.g.* —

Gen. 41¹⁹ οἵας οὐκ εἶδον τοιαύτας.   Ex. 9¹⁸, ²⁴, 11⁶ ἥτις τοιαύτη οὐ γέγονεν.

k. The habitual repetition of the pronoun in the LXX is a mere Hebraism, though a search among Greek writers might reveal traces of a somewhat similar usage arising independently.   Here are a few instances —

Plat. *Tim.* 28 A ὅτου μὲν οὖν ἂν ὁ δημιουργός . . . τὴν ἰδέαν καὶ δύναμιν αὐτοῦ ἀπεργάζηται, *Parm.* 130 E ὧν τάδε τὰ ἀλλὰ μεταλαμβάνοντα τὰς ἐπωνυμίας αὐτῶν ἴσχειν.   Arist. *Cat.* 5 § 38 οἷον ἐπὶ μὲν τῶν ἄλλων οὐκ ἂν ἔχοι τις τὸ τοιοῦτο προενεγκεῖν.

l. In the N.T. this Hebrew syntax of the relative occurs not infrequently.

Philemon¹² ὃν ἀνέπεμψά σοι αὐτόν.   Gal. 2¹⁰ ὃ καὶ ἐσπούδασα αὐτὸ τοῦτο ποιῆσαι.   Acts 15¹⁷ ἐφ᾽ οὓς ἐπικέκληται τὸ ὄνομά μου ἐπ᾽ αὐτούς.   Mk. 7²⁵ ἧς εἶχε τὸ θυγάτριον αὐτῆς πνεῦμα ἀκάθαρτον. *Cp.* Mk. 1⁷: Lk. 3¹⁶: also Mk. 13¹⁹, 9³.

Instances are most frequent in the very Hebraistic book of Revelation.   See Rev. 3⁸, 7³, ⁹, 13⁸, 20⁸.   *Cp.* i Clem. 21⁹ οὗ ἡ πνοὴ αὐτοῦ ἐν ἡμῖν ἐστίν.

70. ἀνήρ = ἕκαστος.   The use of ἀνήρ as a distributive pronoun is a pure Hebraism.

iv K. 18³¹ πίεται ἀνὴρ τὴν ἄμπελον αὐτοῦ, καὶ ἀνὴρ τὴν συκῆν αὐτοῦ φάγεται.   Jdg. 16⁵ ἡμεῖς δώσομέν σοι ἀνὴρ χιλίους καὶ ἑκατὸν ἀργυρίου.

71. ὅστις for ὅς.   Except in the neuter singular ὅ τι, as in Josh. 24²⁷, and in the expression ἕως ὅτου, as in i K. 22³, or μέχρι ὅτου, which is found only in the *Codex Sinaiticus* version of Tob. 5⁷, ὅστις occurs in Swete's text only in the nominative, singular or plural.   In meaning it is often indistinguishable from ὅς.

Ex. 20² Ἐγώ εἰμι Κύριος . . . ὅστις ἐξήγαγόν σε.   *Cp.* Dan. Θ 6²⁷. Ps. 89⁴ ἡ ἡμέρα ἡ ἐχθὲς ἥτις διῆλθεν.   *Cp.* Nb. 14⁸.   i K. 30¹⁰ διακόσιοι ἄνδρες οἵτινες ἐκάθισαν πέραν τοῦ χειμάρρου.   *Cp.* Ex. 32⁴, ⁹: Nb. 1⁵: i Mac. 13⁴⁸.   Jdg. 21¹² τετρακοσίας νεάνιδας παρθένους, αἵτινες οὐκ ἔγνωσαν ἄνδρα.

Οἵτινες = οἱ occurs several times in Aristeas — §§ 102, 121, 138, 200, 308.

The same use of ὅστις for the simple relative is found in the N.T.,
e.g. —

Col. 3⁵ τὴν πλεονεξίαν, ἥτις ἐστὶν εἰδωλολατρεία.   Acts 8¹⁵ τὸν Πέ-
τρον καὶ Ἰωάννην· οἵτινες καταβάντες κτλ.   i Tim. 6⁹ ἐπιθυμίας
. . . αἵτινες βυθίζουσι τοὺς ἀνθρώπους.   Gal. 4²⁴ ἅτινά ἐστιν ἀλλη-
γορούμενα.

VERBS, 72–84

72. Analytic Tenses. By an Analytic Tense is meant one which
is formed with an auxiliary instead of by an inflexion, as in English
'is coming' for 'comes.' No reader of the LXX can fail to be struck
by the frequency of such forms. It results from the fact that both
languages combine to produce them. They are suggested by the
great use made of the participle in Hebrew, while at the same time
there was a strong tendency towards the employment of such forms
within the Greek language itself. They are to be found in the best
writers, both in prose and poetry, from Homer downwards. Plato
often has recourse to them, partly for the sake of philosophical pre-
cision, and partly, it must be confessed, because in his later style he
preferred two words to one. In the *Laws* πρέπον ἐστί almost altogether displaces πρέπει.

PRESENT

iii K. 20⁵	οὐκ εἶ σὺ ἐσθίων ἄρτον; *Cp.* Is. 10⁸ : Ezk. 36¹³.
iii K. 18¹²	ἐστὶν φοβούμενος.
Nb. 14⁸	ἐστὶν ῥέουσα. *Cp.* iii K. 20¹⁵ : Dan. 2²⁸.
ii Esd. 23²⁴	οὐκ εἰσὶν ἐπιγινώσκοντες.
Prov. 3⁵	ἴσθι πεποιθώς.
Jdg. 11¹⁰	ἔστω ἀκούων.
Dan. O′ 6²⁶	ἔστωσαν προσκυνοῦντες.
ii Chr. 15¹⁶	εἶναι . . . λειτουργοῦσαν.

FUTURE SIMPLE

Gen. 4¹⁴	ἔσομαι στένων καὶ τρέμων. *Cp.* Dan. O′ 6²⁷.
Is. 47⁷	ἔσομαι ἄρχουσα.
Gen. 4¹²	στένων καὶ τρέμων ἔσῃ. *Cp.* Ex. 22²⁵ : Dt. 28²⁹.
Dt. 28²⁹	ἔσῃ . . . ἀδικούμενος.
Nb. 8¹⁹	ἔσται . . . προσεγγίζων. *Cp.* Gen. 18¹⁸.
Mal. 3³	ἔσονται . . . προσάγοντες.
Is. 22²⁴	ἔσονται ἐπικρεμάμενοι.
Ezk. 34²⁹	ἔσονται ἀπολλύμενοι. *Cp.* Dt. 14³³.

SYNTAX

PERFECT

Is. 8¹⁴	πεποιθὼς ᾖς.
Is. 10²⁰, 17⁸	πεποιθότες ὦμεν.
Nb. 22¹²	ἔστιν γὰρ εὐλογημένος.

FUTURE PERFECT

Gen. 43⁹, 44³²	ἡμαρτηκὼς ἔσομαι.
ii K. 22³ : Is. 12², 8¹⁷	πεποιθὼς ἔσομαι (fut. simp. in force).
Sir. 7²⁵	ἔσῃ τετελεκώς.
Is. 58¹⁴	ἔσῃ πεποιθώς.
Is. 17⁷, 22²⁴	πεποιθὼς ἔσται.
Ex. 12⁶	ἔσται ὑμῖν διατετηρημένον.
Is. 32³	ἔσονται πεποιθότες.
Gen. 41³⁶	ἔσται . . . πεφυλαγμένα.

IMPERFECT

Dan. 10²	ἤμην πενθῶν.
Dan. O' 7¹¹	θεωρῶν ἤμην.
Gen. 40¹³	ἦσθα οἰνοχοῶν.
Gen. 37² : Ex. 3¹	ἦν ποιμαίνων . *Cp.* Gen. 39²³, 42⁶ : Nb. 11¹ : Jdg. 16²¹ : Jonah 1¹⁰ : Sus.¹ : i Mac. 6⁴³.
i K. 17³⁴	ποιμαίνων ἦν.
Jer. 4²⁴	ἦν τρέμοντα (*sc.* τὰ ὄρη).
iii K. 18³	ἦν φοβούμενος. *Cp.* Dan. O' 6¹⁸.
Dan. O' 1¹⁶	ἦν . . . ἀναιρούμενος.
Baruch 1¹⁹	ἤμεθα ἀπειθοῦντες.
Dt. 9²⁴	ἀπειθοῦντες ἦτε. *Cp.* Dt. 9²², 31²⁷.
Jdg. 1⁷	ἦσαν συλλέγοντες. *Cp.* Josh. 10²⁶ : i Mac. 11⁴¹

PLUPERFECT

Dan. O' 10⁹	ἤμην πεπτωκώς.
Dan. Θ 10⁹	ἤμην κατανενυγμένος.
ii Chr. 18³⁴	ἦν ἑστηκώς.
i K. 4¹³	ἦν . . . ἐξεστηκυῖα.
Jdg. 8¹¹ : Sus. Θ³⁵	ἦν πεποιθυῖα.
Josh. 7²²	ἦν ἐνκεκρυμμένα.
ii Chr. 5⁸	ἦν διαπεπετακότα.
Tob. 6¹⁸	ἡτοιμασμένη ἦν.
Is. 20⁶	ἦμεν πεποιθότες.
Ex. 39²³	ἦσαν πεποιηκότες αὐτά.

b. Γίγνεσθαι may be used as an auxiliary instead of εἶναι.

Ps. 72¹⁴ ἐγενόμην μεμαστιγωμένος.   Is. 30¹² πεποιθὼς ἐγένου.
Nb. 10³⁴ ἐγένετο σκιάζουσα.   Ps. 125³ ἐγενήθημεν εὐφραινόμενοι.
Ex. 17¹² ἐγένοντο . . . ἐστηριγμέναι.   Sir. 13⁹ ὑποχωρῶν γίνου,
18³³ μὴ γίνου . . . συμβολοκοπῶν.

c. Sometimes the verbal adjective is used in place of the participle.

Is. 18³ ἀκουστὸν ἔσται.   Dt. 4³⁶ ἀκουστὴ ἐγένετο.   Gen. 45² :
Is. 48³ ἀκουστὸν ἐγένετο.   Is. 23⁵ ὅταν δὲ ἀκουστὸν γένηται.
Dt. 30⁵ πλεοναστόν σε ποιήσει.

d. When a causative form is wanted corresponding to ἀκουστὸν γενέσθαι recourse is had to ἀκουστὸν ποιεῖν, *e.g.* —

Sir. 46¹⁷ ἀκουστὴν ἐποίησεν τὴν φωνὴν αὐτοῦ.   Cp. Ps. 105², 142⁸ :
Jer. 27², 38⁷ : Is. 30³⁰, 45²¹, 48⁵, ⁶, ²⁰, 52⁷, 62¹¹.

e. In the N.T. these analytic tenses are relatively even commoner than in the LXX.

PRESENT

Col. 3²	ἐστιν . . . καθήμενος.
ii Cor. 9¹²	ἐστὶ προσαναπληροῦσα.
Col. 1⁶	ἐστὶ καρποφορούμενον καὶ αὐξανόμενον.
Col. 2²³	ἐστι . . . ἔχοντα.
ii Cor. 2¹⁷	ἐσμὲν . . . καπηλεύοντες.
Acts 5²⁵	εἰσὶν . . . ἐστῶτες καὶ διδάσκοντες.
Mt. 5²⁵	ἴσθι εὐνοῶν.

FUTURE SIMPLE

Lk. 5¹¹	ἀνθρώπους ἔσῃ ζωγρῶν.
Acts 7⁶	ἔσται . . . πάροικον.
i Cor. 14¹⁰	ἔσεσθε . . . λαλοῦντες.

PERFECT

Acts 25¹⁰	ἐστώς εἰμι (present in meaning).
Acts 21³³	ἐστὶ πεποιηκώς.
i Cor. 15⁹	ἠλπικότες ἐσμέν.
Hb. 7²¹, ²³	εἰσὶ γεγονότες.
James 5¹⁶	ᾖ πεποιηκώς.
ii Cor. 1¹⁹	πεποιθότες ὦμεν.
Hb. 4²	ἐσμὲν εὐηγγελισμένοι.
Hb. 10¹⁰	ἡγιασμένοι ἐσμέν.
Acts 2¹³	μεμεστωμένοι εἰσί.

FUTURE PERFECT

Hb. 2¹³   ἔσομαι πεποιθώς (from Is. 12² and perfect only in form).

IMPERFECT

Acts 10³⁰, 11⁵   ἤμην προσευχόμενος.   Cp. 22¹⁹, ²⁰ : Gal. 1²².

Lk. 4⁴⁴   ἦν κηρύσσων.   Cp. Lk. 5¹⁶, 23⁸ : Acts 7⁶⁰, 8¹³, ²⁸, 9²⁸, 10²⁴, 12²⁰ : Phil. 2²⁶.

Acts 12⁵   ἦν γινομένη.

Acts 21³   ἦν . . . ἀποφορτιζόμενον.

Acts 16¹²   ἦμεν . . . διατρίβοντες.

Gal. 1²³   ἀκούοντες ἦσαν.   Cp. Acts 1¹⁰.

Acts 1¹³   ἦσαν καταμένοντες.   Cp. Acts 1¹⁴, 2², ⁵, ¹², ⁴² : Mk. 2¹⁸.

f. Besides εἶναι other auxiliaries are used in the N.T. —

ii Cor. 6¹⁴ μὴ γίνεσθε ἑτεροζυγοῦντες.   Col. 1¹⁸ ἵνα γένηται . . . πρωτεύων.   Rev. 3² γίνου γρηγορῶν.   Acts 8¹⁶ βεβαπτισμένοι ὑπῆρχον.

With the last example *cp.* Aristeas § 193 εἰ μὴ πεποιθὼς ὑπάρχοι. The same author has κεχαρισμένος ἔσῃ in § 40 and ἰσχύόν ἐστι in 241.

g. Instances of analytic tenses occur here and there in Josephus, *e.g.* —

B.J. I 31 § 1 καὶ τοῦτο ἦν μάλιστα τάρασσον Ἀντίπατρον.

Ant. II 6 § 7 τί παρόντες εἴημεν.

h. Also in the Apostolic Fathers —

ii Clem. 17⁷ ἔσονται δόξαν δόντες.   Barn. *Ep.* 19⁴ ἔσῃ τρέμων, 19⁶ οὐ μὴ γένῃ ἐπιθυμῶν.   Cp. 19⁹.   Herm. *Past. Vis.* III 4 § 2 ὑπερέχοντες αὐτούς εἰσιν, *Sim.* V 4 § 2 ἔσομαι ἑωρακώς . . . ἀκηκοώς, IX 13 § 2 ἔσῃ . . . φορῶν, *Mdt.* V 2 § 8 ἔσῃ εὑρισκόμενος, *Sim.* IX 1 § 8 εὐθηνοῦν ἦν, IX 4 § 1 ὑποδεδυκυῖαι ἦσαν . . . ὑποδεδύκεισαν.

73. Deliberative Use of the Present Indicative. The deliberative use of the present indicative is not unknown in Latin, especially in Terence, *e.g. Phorm.* 447 quid ago?   *Cp. Heaut.* 343 : *Eun.* 811 : *Ad.* 538. It occurs also in the Greek of the LXX.

Gen. 37³⁰ ἐγὼ δὲ ποῦ πορεύομαι ἔτι ;

So in N.T. —

Jn. 11⁴⁷ τί ποιοῦμεν ; *What is our course ?*

74. The Jussive Future. *a.* The Jussive Future is rare in Attic Greek, and, when it does occur, is regarded as a weak form of imperative. In the LXX, on the other hand, it is very common, and is employed in the most solemn language of legislation. From the nature of the case it is not used in the first person. It may be employed in command or in prohibition. As instances of the former we may take —

Lvt. 19¹⁸ ἀγαπήσεις τὸν πλησίον σου ὡς σεαυτόν. *Cp.* Ex. 34¹⁸, ²⁰ : iii K. 17¹¹. Lvt. 19¹⁹ τὸν νόμον μου φυλάξεσθε. *Cp.* Lvt. 11⁴⁴. Lvt. 19²² καὶ ἐξιλάσεται ὁ ἱερεύς. *Cp.* Lvt. 19²⁰, ²¹.

b. Very often the jussive future follows an imperative.

Gen. 40¹⁴ μνήσθητί μου . . . καὶ ποιήσεις. *Cp.* Gen. 44⁴ : Ex. 7²⁶, 9¹, ¹³ : Nb. 15², ¹⁷ : iii K. 17¹³. Josh. 8⁴ μὴ μακρὰν γίνεσθε . . . καὶ ἔσεσθε πάντες ἕτοιμοι. *Cp.* Nb. 13¹⁸.

c. Of the use of the jussive future in prohibition we have a conspicuous example in the Ten Commandments (Ex. 20¹³⁻¹⁷ : Dt. 5¹⁷⁻²¹) — Οὐ μοιχεύσεις, Οὐ κλέψεις κτλ. So also —

Dt. 6¹⁶ οὐκ ἐκπειράσεις Κύριον τὸν θεόν σου. *Cp.* Nb. 22¹² : Ex. 22²⁸ : Lvt. 19¹²⁻¹⁹.

d. In the case of the jussive future we have οὐ in prohibition, because the formula was originally one of prediction.

e. Occasionally there is a transition from the jussive future to οὐ μή with subjunctive —

Nb. 23²⁵ οὔτε κατάραις καταράσῃ μοι αὐτόν, οὔτε εὐλογῶν μὴ εὐλογήσῃς αὐτόν.

f. In the N.T. the jussive future is often used in passages quoted from the LXX. In Matthew it is employed independently.

Mt. 5⁴⁸ ἔσεσθε οὖν ὑμεῖς τέλειοι, 6⁴⁵ οὐκ ἔσεσθε ὡς οἱ ὑποκριταί, 20²⁶⁻²⁸ οὐχ οὕτως ἔσται ἐν ὑμῖν . . . ἔσται ὑμῶν δοῦλος, 21³ καὶ ἐάν τις ὑμῖν εἴπῃ τι, ἐρεῖτε κτλ.

75. The Optative. *a.* The pure optative, *i.e.* the optative as employed to express a wish, is of frequent occurrence in the LXX, as might be expected from the character of the contents, so much of which is in the form either of aspiration or of imprecation. But the use of the optative where in Latin we should have the historic tenses of the subjunctive is hardly to be found outside of Maccabees.

ii Mac. 3³⁷ τοῦ δὲ βασιλέως ἐπερωτήσαντος τὸν Ἡλιόδωρον, ποῖός τις εἴη ἐπιτήδειος.   iv Mac. 17¹ ἔλεγον δὲ καὶ τῶν δορυφόρων τινες ὡς . . . ἵνα μὴ ψαύσειέν τι τοῦ σώματος αὐτῆς, ἑαυτὴν ἔρριψεν κατὰ τῆς πυρᾶς.

The established practice is for the subjunctive to follow the historic tenses in a final clause —

　　Ex. 1¹¹ ἐπέστησεν . . . ἵνα κακώσωσιν, 9¹⁶ διετηρήθης ἵνα ἐνδείξωμαι. Wisd. 16¹¹ διεσώζοντο, ἵνα μὴ . . . γένωνται.   Cp. 16¹⁸.

Cp. Aristeas §§ 11, 18, 19, 26, 29, 42, 45, 111, 175, 193.

b. In the N.T. also the subjunctive is regularly employed in final clauses after an historic tense, e.g. —

　　Tit. 1⁵ τούτου χάριν ἀπέλιπον σε ἐν Κρήτῃ, ἵνα τὰ λείποντα ἐπιδιορθώσῃ.

c. The pure optative is said to occur 35 times in the N.T., always, except in Philemon²⁰, in the 3d person.

In Luke-Acts the optative is commonly employed in dependent questions, e.g. —

　　Luke 18³⁶ ἐπυνθάνετο τί εἴη τοῦτο,

with which contrast

　　Mk. 14¹¹ ἐζήτει πῶς εὐκαίρως αὐτὸν παραδῷ.

Outside of Acts the optative with εἰ is found only in four passages — i Cor. 14¹⁰, 15³⁷ (εἰ τύχοι): i Pet. 3¹⁴, ¹⁷.

76. Conditional without ἄν. Occasionally we find the apodosis in a conditional sentence devoid of ἄν.

　　Nb. 22³³ καὶ εἰ μὴ ἐξέκλινεν, νῦν οὖν σὲ μὲν ἀπέκτεινα, ἐκείνην δὲ περιεποιησάμην.   Contrast 22²⁹ and compare ii K. 2²⁷.

77. Infinitive of Purpose. The use of the infinitive to express purpose, as in English, is common to all stages of the Greek language, but abounds more in the LXX than in classical Greek.

　　Gen. 37²⁵ ἐκάθισαν δὲ φαγεῖν ἄρτον.   Cp. 39¹⁴, 42⁷, ²⁷, 43²²: Ex. 14¹¹: Nb. 22²⁰: Job 2¹.

Of the use of the infinitive with the article to express purpose we have had occasion to speak already (§ 59).

78. Infinitive of Consequence. This construction is of doubtful propriety in Attic Greek. In the LXX it is much less common than the Infinitive of Purpose.

　　Ex. 11¹ καὶ οὐκ εἰσήκουσεν ἐξαποστεῖλαι τοὺς υἱοὺς Ἰσραήλ.

79. Paucity of Participles. The small use made of participles in the LXX, as compared with classical Greek, is a natural result of the paratactical construction which reigns throughout. The same is the case, though to a less extent, in the N.T. Take for instance —

Mk. 14¹⁶ καὶ ἐξῆλθον οἱ μαθηταί, καὶ ἦλθον εἰς τὴν πόλιν, καὶ εὗρεν καθὼς εἶπεν αὐτοῖς· καὶ ἡτοίμασαν τὸ πάσχα.

The participle has disappeared in the modern language. Doubtless the influence of Biblical Greek was among the causes of its decline.

80. Misuse of the Participle. The misuse of the participle marks a stage of its decline. We find this tendency already manifesting itself in the LXX. Such an anacoluthon indeed as the following —

Ex. 8¹⁵, 9⁷ ἰδὼν δὲ Φαραώ . . . ἐβαρύνθη ἡ καρδία αὐτοῦ

may be passed over, as it might easily be paralleled from the most strictly classical writers. But we find sentences in the LXX in which a participle is the only verb. Sometimes this arises from following the Hebrew as in —

Jdg. 13¹⁹, ²⁰ καὶ Μανῶε καὶ ἡ γυνὴ αὐτοῦ βλέποντες, 14⁴ καὶ ἐν τῷ καιρῷ ἐκείνῳ οἱ ἀλλόφυλοι κυριεύοντες ἐν Ἰσραήλ.

More often it does not, as in —

Ex. 12³⁷ ἀπάραντες δὲ οἱ υἱοὶ Ἰσραήλ, 15¹⁸ κύριος βασιλεύων τὸν αἰῶνα. Jdg. 4¹⁶ καὶ Βαρὰκ διώκων.

Moreover we find a participle coupled with a finite verb by καί. When the subject of the two is the same, it is open to us to say that it is not copulative, but merely emphasizes the verb, as in —

Nb. 21¹¹ καὶ ἐξάραντες (Hb. impf.) ἐξ Ὠβώθ, καὶ παρενέβαλον ἐν Χαλγαεί, 22²³ καὶ ἰδοῦσα ἡ ὄνος . . . καὶ ἐξέκλινεν.

Hardly so however when the subject is different.

Ex. 12³⁰ καὶ ἀναστὰς Φαραώ . . . καὶ ἐγενήθη κραυγή. Nb. 22²³ καὶ ἰδὼν Βαλάκ . . . καὶ ἐφοβήθη Μωάβ.

81. The Intensive Participle. On the other hand there is a cause in operation in the LXX tending to an unnecessary use of participles. For in place of a cognate dative we often find the participle used along with a finite form of the same verb, to convey the intensive force that is accomplished in Hebrew by the addition of the infinitive to the finite verb, e.g. —

Gen. 22¹⁷ εἰ μὴν εὐλογῶν εὐλογήσω σε, καὶ πληθύνων πληθυνῶ τὸ σπέρμα σου. Jdg. 11²⁵ μὴ μαχόμενος ἐμαχέσατο μετὰ Ἰσραὴλ ἢ πολεμῶν ἐπολέμησεν αὐτόν; We might fill pages with instances of this idiom, but a statement of its frequency must suffice. This emphatic use of the participle is a more unmitigated Hebraism than the other forms of the etymological figure. The cognate accusative is quite Greek and the cognate dative is to be found in pure Greek, but we should search in vain among classical authors for the intensive use of the participle. There is a clear instance indeed in Lucian (*Dialogi Marini* IV 3 ἰδὼν εἶδον), but it is interesting to remember that Lucian himself came from the banks of the Euphrates. In Hdt. V 95 αὐτὸς μὲν φεύγων ἐκφεύγει there is a difference of meaning between the participle and the finite verb — *he himself escapes by flight.*

In the N.T. we have one instance, other than a quotation, of this Hebraism, namely —

Eph. 5⁵ ἴστε γινώσκοντες,

but both the reading and the interpretation of this passage are disputed.

82. Other Varieties of the Etymological Figure. In Josh. 17¹³ ἐξολεθρεῦσαι δὲ αὐτοὺς οὐκ ἐξωλέθρευσαν the infinitive absolute of the Hebrew is represented in Greek by the infinitive, instead of by a participle or a cognate dative, so that sheer nonsense is made of the translation.

In another passage, where the Greek departs from our Hebrew, an adjective takes the place of the participle —

Jdg. 5³⁰ οἰκτείρμων οἰκτειρήσει.

Sometimes we find an adverb in place of the participle —

Ex. 15¹ ἐνδόξως γὰρ δεδόξασται.   Nb. 22¹⁷ ἐντίμως γὰρ τιμήσω σε.

Prov. 23¹ νοητῶς νόει, 27²³ γνωστῶς ἐπιγνώσῃ.

The following turns of expression may also be noticed —

Jdg. 11²⁵ ἐν ἀγαθῷ ἀγαθώτερος.   Dt. 18⁸ μερίδα μεμερισμένην. i K. 1¹¹ δώσω αὐτὸν ἐνώπιόν σου δοτόν.

83. Middle and Passive Voices. In later Greek the boundary lines between the middle and passive voices are not clearly demarcated. Even in classical authors we find the future middle used in a passive sense, as it is also in —

Ex. 12¹⁰ οὐκ ἀπολείψεται ἀπ᾽ αὐτοῦ ἕως πρωί, καὶ ὀστοῦν οὐ συντρίψεται ἀπ᾽ αὐτοῦ.

The same seems to be the case with ξυρήσωμαι and ἐξυρήσατο in Jdg. 16¹⁷, ²².

So in N.T. —

i Cor. 6¹¹ ἀλλὰ ἀπελούσασθε, ἀλλὰ ἡγιάσθητε, ἀλλ' ἐδικαιώθητε, 10² καὶ πάντες εἰς τὸν Μωσῆν ἐβαπτίσαντο,

though here Riddell's semi-middle sense of the verb might plausibly be brought in by way of explanation.

Instances of passive form with middle meaning are common in the LXX —

Nb. 22³⁴ ἀποστραφήσομαι I will get me back again.   Jdg. 15⁹ ἐξερίφησαν spread themselves, 16²⁰ ἐκτιναχθήσομαι shake myself, 16²⁶ ἐπιστηριχθήσομαι support myself.   iii K. 17³ κρύβηθι hide thyself, 18¹ πορεύθητι καὶ ὄφθητι τῷ Ἀχαάβ go and shew thyself, 20²⁵ ἐπράθη sold himself.

So in N.T. in Luke 11³⁸ ἐβαπτίσθη is used for ἐβαπτίσατο.

84. Causative Use of the Verb. a. The causative use of the verb which is found in the LXX may be set down with confidence as a Hebraism. Βασιλεύειν according to the Greek language means 'to be king,' but it is frequently employed in the LXX in the sense of 'to make king,' e.g. —

Jdg. 9⁶ ἐβασίλευσαν τὸν Ἀβειμέλεχ.   i K. 8²² βασίλευσον αὐτοῖς βασιλέα, 15¹¹ ἐβασίλευσα τὸν Σαοὺλ εἰς βασιλέα.

There are all together thirty-six occurrences of the word in this causative sense.

b. Classical Greek again knows βδελύσσεσθαι in the sense of 'to loathe' or 'abominate,' but not βδελύσσειν in the sense of 'to make abominable,' as in —

Ex. 5²¹ ἐβδελύξατε τὴν ὀσμὴν ἡμῶν ἐναντίον Φαραώ.   Lvt. 11⁴³ καὶ οὐ μὴ βδελύξητε τὰς ψυχὰς ὑμῶν.   Cp. Lvt. 20²⁵: i Mac. 1⁴⁸.

c. Still more strange to classical Greek is the sense of 'to make to sin' often imposed upon ἐξαμαρτάνειν, e.g. —

iv K. 17²¹ καὶ ἐξήμαρτεν αὐτοὺς ἁμαρτίαν μεγάλην.

This is the prevailing sense of the word in the LXX, which is found all together twenty-eight times, mostly in the phrase ὃς ἐξήμαρτεν τὸν Ἰσραήλ.

d. In this causative use of the verb is to be found the explanation of Ex. 14²⁵ καὶ ἤγαγεν αὐτοὺς μετὰ βίας, where the R.V. margin has 'made them to drive.' Other similar instances are —

Ex. 13¹⁸ ἐκύκλωσεν = he led round. i K. 4³ κατὰ τί ἔπταισεν ἡμᾶς κύριος σήμερον; Ps. 142¹¹ ζήσεις με.

85. Reduplication of Words. In Greek we are accustomed to reduplication of syllables, but not to reduplication of words. This primitive device of language is resorted to in the LXX, in imitation of the Hebrew, for at least three different purposes —

        (1) intensification,
        (2) distribution,
        (3) universalisation.

(1) The intensifying use.

σφόδρα σφόδρα Gen. 30⁴³: Ex. 1⁷,¹²: Nb. 14⁷: Ezk. 9⁹: Judith 4².
σφόδρα σφοδρῶς Gen. 7¹⁹: Josh. 3¹⁶.

To the same head may be assigned —

Ex. 8¹⁴ συνήγαγον αὐτοὺς θιμωνιὰς θιμωνιάς. Dt. 28⁴³ ὁ προσήλυτος ὁ ἐν σοὶ ἀναβήσεται ἄνω ἄνω, σὺ δὲ καταβήσῃ κάτω κάτω.

In all the above instances perhaps the kind of intensification involved is that of a repeated process.

(2) The distributive use.

εἷς εἷς i Chr. 24⁶.
δύο δύο Gen. 6¹⁹, 7³: Sir. 36¹⁵.
ἑπτὰ ἑπτά Gen. 7³.
χιλίους ἐκ φυλῆς, χιλίους ἐκ φυλῆς Nb. 31⁶.
τὸ πρωὶ πρωί i Chr. 9²⁷.
ἐργασίᾳ καὶ ἐργασίᾳ ii Chr. 34¹³.

In pure Greek such ideas would be expressed by the use of ἀνά or κατά. Sometimes we find κατά employed in the LXX along with the reduplication, as in —

Dt. 7²² κατὰ μικρὸν μικρόν. Zech. 12¹² κατὰ φυλὰς φυλάς.

The idea 'year by year' is expressed in many different ways —

ἐνιαυτὸν κατ᾽ ἐνιαυτόν Dt. 14²¹: i K. 1⁷: ii Chr. 24⁵.
κατ᾽ ἐνιαυτὸν ἐνιαυτόν i K. 7¹⁶.
ἐνιαυτὸν ἐξ ἐνιαυτοῦ Dt. 15²⁰.
τὸ κατ᾽ ἐνιαυτὸν ἐνιαυτῷ iii K. 10²⁸.
τὸ κατ᾽ ἐνιαυτὸν ἐνιαυτόν ii Chr. 9²⁴.

(3) The universalising use.

ἄνθρωπος ἄνθρωπος = whatsoever man Lvt. 17³, ⁸, ¹⁰, ¹³, 18⁶, 20⁹, 22¹⁸ : Ezk. 14⁴, ⁷.

ἀνδρὶ ἀνδρί Lvt. 15³.

Of the above three uses the distributive is the only one which is to be found in the N.T.

Mk. 6⁷ δύο δύο, 6³⁹ συμπόσια συμπόσια, 6⁴⁰ πρασιαὶ πρασιαί.

So also in the *Pastor* of Hermas —

> *Sim.* VIII 2 § 8 ἦλθον τάγματα τάγματα, 4 § 2 ἔστησαν τάγματα τάγματα.

86. Expressions of Time. *a.* 'Year after year' is expressed in ii K. 21¹ by a nominative absolute ἐνιαυτὸς ἐχόμενος ἐνιαυτοῦ without any pretence of grammar.

b. The use of the word 'day' in vague expressions of time is a Hebraism, *e.g.* —

Gen. 40⁴ ἡμέρας = for some time. *Cp.* Dan. O' 11⁹. Jdg. 15¹ μεθ᾽ ἡμέρας = after some time. *Cp.* iii K. 17⁷. iii K. 18¹ μεθ᾽ ἡμέρας πολλάς = after a long time.

c. 'Day by day' (Hb. *day, day*) is expressed in Gen. 39¹⁰ by ἡμέραν ἐξ ἡμέρας (*cp.* Lat. diem ex die). In Esther 3⁴ καθ᾽ ἑκάστην ἡμέραν is correctly used as the Greek equivalent for the phrase *day and day*, which St. Paul (ii Cor. 4¹⁶) has reproduced word for word in the form ἡμέρᾳ καὶ ἡμέρᾳ.

d. The use of 'yesterday and the day before' as a general expression for past time = *heretofore* is a Hebraism which presents itself in the LXX under a variety of slight modifications.

ἐχθὲς καὶ τρίτην i K. 4⁷, 10¹¹ : ii K. 3¹⁷, 5² : i Chr. 11².
ἐχθὲς καὶ τρίτην ἡμέραν Gen. 31², ⁵ : Ex. 5⁷, ¹⁴ : Josh. 4¹⁸ : i K. 14²¹, 19⁷, 21⁵ : i Mac. 9⁴⁴.
ἐχθὲς καὶ τρίτης Ruth 2¹¹ : iv K. 13⁵ : Sus. Θ¹⁵.
ἀπ᾽ ἐχθὲς καὶ τρίτης ἡμέρας Josh. 3⁴.
πρὸ τῆς ἐχθὲς καὶ τρίτης Dt. 19⁴.
πρὸ τῆς ἐχθὲς καὶ πρὸ τῆς τρίτης Ex. 21²⁹.
πρὸ τῆς ἐχθὲς καὶ πρὸ τῆς τρίτης ἡμέρας Ex. 21³⁶.
πρὸ τῆς ἐχθὲς οὐδὲ πρὸ τῆς τρίτης Dt. 4⁴², 19⁶.
πρὸ τῆς ἐχθὲς οὐδὲ πρὸ τῆς τρίτης ἡμέρας Ex. 4¹⁰.

In Joshua 20⁵, which occurs only in the *Codex Alexandrinus*, we have ἀπ' ἐχθὲς καὶ τρίτην, where ἐχθὲς-καὶ-τρίτην is treated as a single indeclinable noun.

e. 'Just at that time' is expressed variously as follows —

αὐθωρί Dan. O' 3¹⁵.

αὐτῇ τῇ ὥρᾳ i Esd. 8⁶⁵ : Dan. 3⁵, Θ 3¹⁵. *Cp.* Acts 22¹³.

ἐν αὐτῇ τῇ ὥρᾳ Dan. Θ 5⁵. *Cp.* Lk. 12¹², 13³¹, 20¹⁹.

ἐν αὐτῇ τῇ ὥρᾳ ἐκείνη Dan. O' 5⁵.

ἐν αὐτῷ τῷ καιρῷ Tob. 3¹⁷. *Cp.* Lk. 13¹.

87. Pleonastic Use of ἐκεῖ and ἐκεῖθεν. Just as a personal pronoun is supplied after the relative (§ 69), so a demonstrative adverb of place is supplied after a relative adverb or after some phrase equivalent to one.

Gen. 33¹⁹ οὗ ἔστησεν ἐκεῖ τὴν σκηνὴν αὐτοῦ. *Cp.* 39²⁰, 40³ : Ex. 21¹³. Ex. 20²⁴ οὗ ἐὰν ἐπονομάσω τὸ ὄνομά μου ἐκεῖ. Dan. Θ 9⁷ οὗ διέσπειρας αὐτοὺς ἐκεῖ. iii K. 17¹⁹ ἐν ᾧ αὐτὸς ἐκάθητο ἐκεῖ. *Cp.* Gen. 39²⁰ : Ex. 12¹³. Gen. 31¹³ ἐν τῷ τόπῳ ᾧ ἤλειψάς μοι ἐκεῖ στήλην. Nb. 14²⁴ εἰς ἣν εἰσῆλθεν ἐκεῖ. *Cp.* 15¹⁸, 35²⁶ : Dt. 4²⁷. Ex. 8²² ἐφ' ἧς οὐκ ἔσται ἐκεῖ. iv K. 1⁴ ἡ κλίνη ἐφ' ἧς ἀνέβης ἐκεῖ. Dt. 9²⁸ ὅθεν ἐξήγαγες ἡμᾶς ἐκεῖθεν. Nb. 23¹³ ἐξ ὧν οὐκ ὄψῃ αὐτὸν ἐκεῖθεν. Dan. O' 9⁷ εἰς ἃς διεσκόρπισας αὐτοὺς ἐκεῖ.

This idiom, which is thoroughly Hebrew, is to be explained on the same principle as in § 69. In the N.T. it is found only in Revelation —

Rev. 12⁶ ὅπου ἔχει ἐκεῖ τόπον, 12¹⁴ ὅπου τρέφεται ἐκεῖ, 17⁹ ὅπου ἡ γυνὴ κάθηται ἐπ' αὐτῶν (= ἐκεῖ).

88. πᾶς with οὐ and μή. a. The use of πᾶς with a negative particle, where in classical Greek οὐδείς or μηδείς would be employed, is a Hebraism, even though in certain cases the resulting expression may be paralleled from pure Greek usage.

The πᾶς may either precede or follow the negative (οὐ, μή, μηδέ, οὐ μή) without difference of meaning.

b. We will first take instances from the LXX where the πᾶς precedes the negative.

Ex. 12⁴³ πᾶς ἀλλογενὴς οὐκ ἔδεται ἀπ' αὐτοῦ. *Cp.* 12⁴⁸ : Ezek. 44⁹. Dan. O' 5⁹ πᾶς ἄνθρωπος οὐ δύναται. *Cp.* Dan. O' 2¹⁰. Hbk. 2¹⁹ πᾶν πνεῦμα οὐκ ἔστιν ἐν αὐτῷ. i Mac. 2⁶¹ πάντες . . . οὐκ ἀσθενήσουσιν. Ex. 22²² πᾶσαν χήραν καὶ ὀρφανὸν οὐ κακώσετε. Jer. 17²² πᾶν ἔργον οὐ ποιήσετε. *Cp.* Ex. 12¹⁶, ²⁰ : Nb. 28¹⁸ : Jdg. 13¹⁴.

So in N.T. —

Rom. 10¹² πᾶς ὁ πιστεύων ἐπ' αὐτῷ οὐ καταισχυνθήσεται. *Cp.* Eph. 4²⁹, 5⁵. Rev. 18²² πᾶς τεχνίτης . . . οὐ μὴ εὑρεθῇ ἐν σοὶ ἔτι. ii Pet. 1²⁰ πᾶσα προφητεία γραφῆς ἰδίας ἐπιλύσεως οὐ γίνεται. i Jn. 2²¹ πᾶν ψεῦδος ἐκ τῆς ἀληθείας οὐκ ἔστι. *Cp.* i Jn. 3⁶, ¹⁰, ¹⁵, 4³, 5¹⁸ : Rev. 22³.

c. In the following passages of the LXX the πᾶς follows the negative —

Ps. 142² οὐ δικαιωθήσεται ἐνώπιόν σου πᾶς ζῶν. Eccl. 1⁹ οὐκ ἔστιν πᾶν πρόσφατον ὑπὸ τὸν ἥλιον. Ex. 20¹⁰ : Dt. 5¹⁴ οὐ ποιήσετε ἐν αὐτῇ πᾶν ἔργον. *Cp.* Ex. 20¹⁶. ii K. 15¹¹ οὐκ ἔγνωσαν πᾶν ῥῆμα. Tob. 12¹¹ οὐ μὴ κρύψω ἀφ' ὑμῶν πᾶν ῥῆμα. Ps. 33¹¹ οὐκ ἐλαττωθήσονται παντὸς ἀγαθοῦ. Jdg. 13⁴ μὴ φάγῃς πᾶν ἀκάθαρτον. Tob. 4⁷ μὴ ἀποστρέψῃς τὸ πρόσωπόν σου ἀπὸ παντὸς πτωχοῦ.

So in N.T. —

Rom. 3²⁰ ἐξ ἔργων νόμου οὐ δικαιωθήσεται πᾶσα σάρξ. *Cp.* Gal. 2¹⁶ : Mt. 24²². Lk. 1³⁷ οὐκ ἀδυνατήσει παρὰ τοῦ Θεοῦ πᾶν ῥῆμα. Acts 10¹⁴ οὐδέποτε ἔφαγον πᾶν κοινόν. i Cor. 1²⁹ ὅπως μὴ καυχήσηται πᾶσα σάρξ. Rev. 21²⁷ οὐ μὴ εἰσέλθῃ εἰς αὐτὴν πᾶν κοινόν.

PREPOSITIONS, 89–98

89. Prominence of Prepositions. The prominence of prepositions in the LXX is partly a characteristic of later Greek generally and partly due to the careful following of the Hebrew. But while prepositions are employed to express relations for which in classical Greek cases would have been thought sufficient, there is at the same time a tendency to blur some of the nice distinctions between the uses of the same preposition with different cases.

90. εἰς. *a.* εἰς in classical Greek denotes motion or direction : in Biblical Greek it denotes equally rest or position, and may be translated by ' at ' or ' in ' as well as by ' to,' *e.g.* —

Gen. 37¹⁷ πορευθῶμεν εἰς Δωθάειμ . . . καὶ εὗρεν αὐτοὺς εἰς Δωθάειμ. Josh. 7²² ἔδραμον εἰς τὴν σκηνὴν . . . καὶ ταῦτα ἦν ἐνκεκρυμμένα εἰς τὴν σκηνήν. Jdg. 14¹ καὶ κατέβη Σαμψὼν εἰς Θαμνάθα, καὶ εἶδεν γυναῖκα εἰς Θαμνάθα.

For examples of the former meaning only we may take —

Gen. 42^{32} ὁ δὲ μικρότερος . . . εἰς γῆν Χανάαν.   Nb. 25^{33} τὴν γῆν εἰς ἣν ὑμεῖς κατοικεῖτε.   Judith 16^{23} ἀπέθανεν εἰς Βαιτυλουά.

b. In the N.T. εἰς denoting rest or position is very common.

Mk. 2^1 εἰς οἶκον = at home.   Cp. Lk. 9^{61}: Mk. 10^{10}.   Mk. 13^3 καθημένου εὐτοῦ εἰς τὸ ὄρος τῶν ἐλαιῶν.   Jn. 1^{18} ὁ ὢν εἰς τὸν κόλπον τοῦ παι͵ ός.   Acts 21^{13} ἀποθανεῖν εἰς Ἰερουσαλήμ.

Cp. also Eph. 3^{16}: i Pet. 3^{20}, 5^{12}: Mk. 1$^{9,\ 39}$, 13^9: Lk. 4^{23}, 11^7: Jn. 9^7, 20^7: Acts 7^4, 8^{40}, 25^4.

The obliteration of the distinction between rest and motion is one of the marks of declining Greek. In the modern language εἰς has usurped the functions both of ἐν and πρός.

c. The use of εἰς with the accusative after εἶναι and γενέσθαι as practically equivalent to the nominative may safely be regarded as a Hebraism.

d. i Chr. 11^{21} ἦν αὐτοῖς εἰς ἄρχοντα, 17^7 εἶναι εἰς ἡγούμενον.   iii K. 20^2 ἔσται μοι εἰς κῆπον λαχάνων.   Cp. Gen. 48^{19}: i Chr. 11^6.   i K. 17^9 ἐσόμεθα ὑμῖν εἰς δούλους.   Jer. 38^{33} ἔσομαι αὐτοῖς εἰς θεὸν, καὶ αὐτοὶ ἔσονταί μοι εἰς λαόν.   Cp. Jer. 38^1: Gen. 48^{19}: ii K. 7^{14}. Gen. 2^7 ἐγένετο ὁ ἄνθρωπος εἰς ψυχὴν ζῶσαν.   Ex. 2^{10} ἐγενήθη αὐτῇ εἰς υἱόν.   i K. 4^9 γένεσθε εἰς ἄνδρας.

πρός in one passage takes the place of εἰς.

Sir. 46^4 μία ἡμέρα ἐγενήθη πρὸς δύο.

e. In the New Testament this idiom occurs both in quotations from the Old and otherwise.

i Jn. 5^8 καὶ οἱ τρεῖς εἰς τὸ ἕν εἰσιν.   Lk. 3^5 ἔσται τὰ σκολιὰ εἰς εὐθείας (Is. 40^4).   ii Cor. 6^{18} ἔσεσθέ μοι εἰς υἱούς καὶ θυγατέρας (ii K. 7^8: Is. 43^6).   Mt. 19^5 ἔσονται οἱ δύο εἰς σάρκα μίαν (Gen. 2^{24}).   Mt. 21^{42} ἐγενήθη εἰς κεφαλὴν γωνίας (Ps. 117^{22}). Lk. 13^{19} ἐγένετο εἰς δένδρον.   Cp. Rev. 8^{11}.   Jn. 16^{20} ἡ λύπη ὑμῶν εἰς χαρὰν γενήσεται.

The same usage is to be found also in the Apostolic Fathers —

Herm. Past. Sim. IX 13 § 5 ἔσονται εἰς ἕν πνεῦμα, εἰς ἕν σῶμα. i Clem. 11^2 εἰς κρίμα καὶ εἰς σημείωσιν . . . γίνονται.   Ign. Eph. 11^1 ἵνα μὴ ἡμῖν εἰς κρίμα γένηται.

f. The employment of εἰς to express the object or destination of a thing might easily be paralleled from classical Greek, but its frequent use in the LXX is due to its convenience as a translation of the corresponding Hebrew.

Gen. 34¹² καὶ δώσετέ μοι τὴν παῖδα ταύτην εἰς γυναῖκα.   Ps. 104¹⁷ εἰς δοῦλον ἐπράθη Ἰωσήφ.   iii K. 19¹⁵ χρίσεις τὸν Ἀζαὴλ εἰς βασιλέα. Gen. 12² ποιήσω σε εἰς ἔθνος μέγα.

When the verb is active and transitive, as in all but the second of the above instances, εἰς might be dispensed with as far as Greek is concerned.   When a verb of being is employed, this use runs into the preceding —

Gen. 1²⁹ ὑμῖν ἔσται εἰς βρῶσιν, 1¹⁴ ἔστωσαν εἰς σημεῖα.

g. The use of εἰς with the accusative, where classical Greek would simply have employed a dative, is shown by the Papyri to have been a feature of the vernacular Greek of Alexandria.

Ex. 9²¹ ὃς δὲ μὴ προσέσχεν τῇ διανοίᾳ εἰς τὸ ῥῆμα κυρίου κτλ.

So in N.T. —

i Cor. 16¹ τῆς λογίας τῆς εἰς τοὺς ἁγίους (*the collection for the saints*).

91. ἐν. *a.* Although ἐν was destined ultimately to disappear before εἰς, yet in Biblical Greek we find it in the plenitude of its power, as expressing innumerable relations, some of which seem to the classical student to be quite beyond its proper sphere.   One principal use may be summed up under the title of " The ἐν of Accompanying Circumstances."   This includes the instrumental use, but goes far beyond it.   Under this aspect ἐν invades the domain of μετά and σύν. In most cases it may be rendered by the English ' with.'

Hos. 1⁷ σώσω αὐτοὺς ἐν κυρίῳ θεῷ αὐτῶν, καὶ οὐ σώσω αὐτοὺς ἐν τόξῳ οὐδὲ ἐν ῥομφαίᾳ οὐδὲ ἐν πολέμῳ οὐδὲ ἐν ἵπποις οὐδὲ ἐν ἱππεῦσιν.   Cp. i K. 17⁴⁵, ⁴⁷ : i Mac. 3¹². Ex. 6¹ ἐν γὰρ χειρὶ κραταιᾷ κτλ. (But in Ex. 3¹⁹ we have ἐὰν μὴ μετὰ χειρὸς κραταιᾶς.)   Cp. Ex. 3²⁰ : Jdg. 15¹⁵, ¹⁶. Jdg. 14¹⁸ εἰ μὴ ἠροτριάσατε ἐν τῇ δαμάλει μου.   Cp. iii K. 19¹⁹. iv K. 18¹⁷ ἐν δυνάμει βαρείᾳ. In the parallel passage Is. 36² μετὰ δυνάμεως πολλῆς.   i Mac. 4⁶ ὤφθη Ἰούδας . . . ἐν τρισχιλίοις ἀνδράσιν.

So in N.T. —

i Cor. 4²¹ ἐν ῥάβδῳ ἔλθω πρὸς ὑμᾶς ;   *Cp.* i K. 17⁴³ : Ps. 2⁹. Eph. 6² ἐντολὴ πρώτη ἐν ἐπαγγελίᾳ.   ii Pet. 3¹⁶ ἐν ἀνθρώπου φωνῇ. Mt. 9³⁴ ἐν τῷ ἄρχοντι τῶν δαιμονίων ἐκβάλλει τὰ δαιμόνια.   *Cp.* Mt. 12²⁴, 25¹⁶.   Mt. 26⁵² ἐν μαχαίρᾳ ἀπολοῦνται.

b. The ἐν of accompanying circumstances is not wholly foreign to classical Greek, though the extended use made of it in Biblical diction is.

Eur. *Tro.* 817 ὦ χρυσέαις ἐν οἰνοχόαις ἁβρὰ βαίνων.

c. In another of its Biblical uses ἐν becomes indistinguishable from εἰς, as in —

Ex. 4²¹ πάντα τὰ τέρατα ἃ ἔδωκα ἐν ταῖς χερσίν σου.   Jdg. 13¹ παρέδωκεν αὐτοὺς Κύριος ἐν χειρὶ Φυλιστιείμ. *Cp.* Jdg. 15¹², ¹³, 16²³, ²⁴. Is. 37¹⁰ οὐ μὴ παραδοθῇ Ἱερουσαλὴμ ἐν χειρὶ βασιλέως, while the parallel passage in iv K. 19¹⁰ has εἰς χεῖρας βασιλέως.   Tob. 5⁵ πορευθῆναι ἐν Ῥάγοις. *Cp.* Tob. 6⁶, 9².

So in N.T. —

ii Cor. 8¹⁶ χάρις δὲ τῷ Θεῷ τῷ διδόντι τὴν αὐτὴν σπουδὴν ὑπὲρ ὑμῶν ἐν τῇ καρδίᾳ Τίτου.   Mt. 14³ ἔθετο ἐν φυλακῇ.   Jn. 3³⁵ πάντα δέδωκεν ἐν τῇ χειρὶ αὐτοῦ.   Rev. 11¹¹ πνεῦμα ζωῆς ἐκ τοῦ Θεοῦ εἰσῆλθεν ἐν αὐτοῖς.

92. ἀπό. *a.* ἀπό in the LXX is often little more than a sign of the genitive, like our English ' of,' provided that the genitive be partitive.

Ex. 12⁴⁶ καὶ ὀστοῦν οὐ συντρίψετε ἀπ᾽ αὐτοῦ.   Josh. 9⁸ οὐκ ἦν ῥῆμα ἀπὸ πάντων ὧν ἐνετείλατο Μωυσῆς τῷ Ἰησοῖ ὃ οὐκ ἀνέγνω Ἰησοῦς. iii K. 18¹³ ἔκρυψα ἀπὸ τῶν προφητῶν Κυρίου ἑκατὸν ἄνδρας.   Joel 2²⁸ ἐκχεῶ ἀπὸ τοῦ πνεύματός μου.   ii Esd. 11² εἷς ἀπὸ ἀδελφῶν μου.

So in N.T. —

Lk. 6¹³ ἐκλεξάμενος ἀπ᾽ αὐτῶν δώδεκα.   Jn. 21¹⁰ ἐνέγκατε ἀπὸ τῶν ὀψαρίων ὧν ἐπιάσατε νῦν.

b. ἀπό = ' by reason of ' is another unclassical use which occurs in the LXX.

Gen. 41³¹ καὶ οὐκ ἐπιγνωσθήσεται ἡ εὐθηνία ἐπὶ τῆς γῆς ἀπὸ τοῦ λιμοῦ. Ex. 2²³ καὶ κατεστέναξαν οἱ υἱοὶ Ἰσραὴλ ἀπὸ τῶν ἔργων, 3⁷ καὶ τῆς κραυγῆς αὐτῶν ἀκήκοα ἀπὸ τῶν ἐργοδιωκτῶν.   Ps. 11⁶ ἀπὸ τῆς ταλαιπωρίας τῶν πτωχῶν . . . ἀναστήσομαι.   Sir. 20⁶ ἔστιν μισητὸς ἀπὸ πολλῆς λαλιᾶς.   Nahum 1⁶ αἱ πέτραι διεθρύβησαν ἀπ᾽ αὐτοῦ.

In this way ἀπό becomes = ὑπό, as in Dan. Οʹ 1¹⁸.

So in N.T. —

Hb. 5⁷ εἰσακουσθεὶς ἀπὸ τῆς εὐλαβείας.   Lk. 19³ οὐκ ἠδύνατο ἀπὸ
τοῦ ὄχλου, 24⁴¹ ἀπιστούντων αὐτῶν ἀπὸ τῆς χαρᾶς.   Cp. Acts 12¹⁴,
22¹¹.   Jn. 21⁶ οὐκέτι αὐτὸ ἑλκύσαι ἴσχυον ἀπὸ τοῦ πλήθους τῶν
ἰχθύων.

Of ἀπό = ὑπό see instances in Lk. 9²², 17²⁵ : Acts 20⁹.

c. The combination ἀπό . . . ἕως is a Hebraism.   It may be rendered "from . . . unto," as in —

  Dt. 8³⁵ ἀπὸ ἴχνους τῶν ποδῶν σου ἕως τῆς κορυφῆς σου,

or "both . . . and," as in —

  Ex. 9²⁵ ἀπὸ ἀνθρώπου . . . ἕως κτήνους.

Sometimes καί precedes the ἕως —

  Jdg. 15⁵ ἀπὸ . . . καὶ ἕως . . . καὶ ἕως both . . . and . . . and.
  Cp. Sir. 40³ : Jer. 27³.

93. μετά. μετά with genitive = 'in dealing with' is a Hebraism.

  Jdg. 15³ ὅτι ποιῶ ἐγὼ μετ' αὐτῶν πονηρίαν.

So in N.T. —

  Lk. 10³⁷ ὁ ποιήσας τὸ ἔλεος μετ' αὐτοῦ : Acts 14²⁷.   Cp. Herm.
  Past. Sim. v 1 § 1 : i Clem. 61³.

94. ὑπέρ. a. The frequent use of ὑπέρ in the LXX to express comparison is due to the fact that the Hebrew language has no special
form for the comparative degree.   We therefore sometimes find the
LXX representing the original by the positive with ὑπέρ.

  Ruth 4¹⁵ ἥ ἐστιν ἀγαθή σοι ὑπὲρ ἑπτὰ υἱούς.   Cp. i K. 1⁸, 15²⁸ : iii K.
  20² : ii Chr. 21¹⁴.   i K. 9² ὑψηλὸς ὑπὲρ πᾶσαν τὴν γῆν.   i Chr.
  4⁹ ἔνδοξος ὑπὲρ τοὺς ἀδελφοὺς αὐτοῦ.   Sir. 24²⁰ ὑπὲρ μέλι γλυκύ.
  Ezk. 5¹ ῥομφαίαν ὀξεῖαν ὑπὲρ ξυρὸν κουρέως.

b. More often however the comparative is used, but the construction with ὑπέρ still retained.

  Jdg. 15² ἀγαθωτέρα ὑπὲρ αὐτήν.   Cp. Jdg. 11²⁵.   Jdg. 18²⁶ δυνατώ-
  τεροί εἰσιν ὑπὲρ αὐτόν.   Ruth 3¹² ἐγγίων ὑπὲρ ἐμέ.   iii K. 19⁴
  κρείσσων . . . ὑπὲρ τοὺς πατέρας.   Cp. Sir. 30¹⁷.   Hbk. 1⁸ ὀξύ-
  τεροι ὑπὲρ λύκους.   Dan. O' 1²⁰ σοφωτέρους δεκαπλασίως ὑπὲρ
  τοὺς σοφιστάς.

SYNTAX

c. ὑπέρ is employed in the same way after verbs —

Ex. 1⁹ ἰσχύει ὑπὲρ ἡμᾶς.   i K. 1⁵ τὴν Ἄνναν ἠγάπα Ἐλκανὰ ὑπὲρ ταύτην.   Ps. 39¹³ ἐπληθύνθησαν ὑπὲρ τὰς τρίχας τῆς κεφαλῆς μου. i Chr. 19¹² ἐὰν κρατήσῃ ὑπὲρ ἐμὲ Σύρος.   Jer. 5³ ἐστερέωσαν ... ὑπὲρ πέτραν, 16¹² ὑμεῖς ἐπονηρεύσασθε ὑπὲρ τοὺς πατέρας ὑμῶν. Cp. 17²³. Jer. 26²³ πληθύνει ὑπὲρ ἀκρίδα.   Dan. O′ 3²² ἡ κάμινος ἐξεκαύθη ὑπὲρ τὸ πρότερον ἑπταπλασίως.

d. So in N.T. —
after a comparative —

Lk. 16⁸ φρονιμώτεροι ὑπὲρ τοὺς υἱοὺς τοῦ φωτός.   Hb. 4¹² τομώτερος ὑπὲρ πᾶσαν μάχαιραν.

after a verb —

Gal. 1¹⁴ προέκοπτον . . . ὑπὲρ πολλούς.   Mt. 10³⁷ ὁ φιλῶν πατέρα ἢ μητέρα ὑπὲρ ἐμέ.
Cp. Herm. Past. Mdt. V 1 § 6 ἡ μακροθυμία γλυκυτάτη ἐστὶν ὑπὲρ τὸ μέλι.   Mart. Polyc. 18 δοκιμώτερα ὑπὲρ χρυσίον ὀστᾶ αὐτοῦ.

95. ἐπί. **a.** ἐπί with the accusative is used of rest as well as of motion.

Gen. 41¹⁷ ἑστάναι ἐπὶ τὸ χεῖλος τοῦ ποταμοῦ.   Ex. 10¹⁴ καὶ ἀνήγαγεν αὐτὴν (τὴν ἀκρίδα) ἐπὶ πᾶσαν γῆν Αἰγύπτου, καὶ κατέπαυσεν ἐπὶ πάντα τὰ ὅρια Αἰγύπτου πολλὴ σφόδρα.   Jdg. 16²⁷ ἐπὶ τὸ δῶμα = upon the roof.

b. ἐπί is sometimes used to reinforce an accusative of duration of time.

Jdg. 14¹⁷ καὶ ἔκλαυσεν πρὸς αὐτὸν ἐπὶ τὰς ἑπτὰ ἡμέρας ἃς ἦν αὐτοῖς ὁ πότος.

c. In Josh. 25¹⁰ we find μέγαν ἐπὶ τοῦ ἰδεῖν where in classical Greek we should have only μέγαν ἰδεῖν.

d. In the N.T. also ἐπί with the accusative is used of rest or position —

ii Cor. 3¹⁵ κάλυμμα ἐπὶ τὴν καρδίαν αὐτῶν κεῖται.   Mk. 2¹⁴ καθήμενον ἐπὶ τὸ τελώνιον. Cp. Lk. 5²⁷.   Mk. 4³⁸ ἐπὶ τὸ προσκεφάλαιον καθεύδων.   Mt. 14²⁸ περιπατῶν ἐπὶ τὴν θάλασσαν (in Jn. 6¹⁹ περιπατοῦντα ἐπὶ τῆς θαλάσσης).   Lk. 2²⁵ πνεῦμα ἅγιον ἦν ἐπ᾽ αὐτόν. Cp. Lk. 2⁴⁰.   Jn. 1³² ἔμεινεν ἐπ᾽ αὐτόν.

96. παρά. **a.** παρά naturally lends itself to the expression of comparison, and is so used occasionally in the best Greek, e.g. Thuc. I 23

§ 4: Xen. *Mem.* I 4 § 14: Hdt. VII 103. It is therefore not surprising that it should have been employed by the translators in the same way as ὑπέρ.

Ex. 18¹¹ μέγας Κύριος παρὰ πάντας τοὺς θεούς. *Cp.* Ps. 134⁵: Dan. O′ 11¹². Nb. 12³ καὶ ὁ ἄνθρωπος Μωυσῆς πραὺς σφόδρα παρὰ πάντας τοὺς ἀνθρώπους. Dan. O′ 1¹⁰ ἀσθενῆ παρὰ τοὺς συντρεφομένους ὑμῖν (Θ has σκυθρωπὰ παρὰ τὰ παιδάρια τὰ συνήλικα ὑμῶν). *Cp.* O′ 1¹³. Dan. Θ 7⁷ διάφορον περισσῶς παρὰ πάντα τὰ θήρια. i Esd. 4³⁵ ἰσχυροτέρα παρὰ πάντα. Dan. O′ 11¹³ μείζονα παρὰ τὴν πρώτην (Θ has πολὺν ὑπὲρ τὸν πρότερον). Dt. 7⁷ ὑμεῖς γάρ ἐστε ὀλιγοστοὶ παρὰ πάντα τὰ ἔθνη. Gen. 43³⁴ ἐμεγαλύνθη δὲ ἡ μερὶς Βενιαμεὶν παρὰ τὰς μερίδας πάντων. Ps. 8⁶ ἠλάττωσας αὐτὸν βραχύ τι παρ᾽ ἀγγέλους.

b. In the N.T. παρά after a comparative is abundant in Hebrews — 1⁴, 3³, 9²³, 11⁴, 12²⁴.

We find it after a positive and after a comparative in Luke —

Lk. 13² ἁμαρτωλοὶ παρὰ πάντας τοὺς Γαλιλαίους, 3¹³ μηδὲν πλέον παρὰ τὸ διατεταγμένον ὑμῖν πράσσετε,

and after verbs in —

Rom. 14⁵ ὃς μὲν κρίνει ἡμέραν παρ᾽ ἡμέραν.   Hb. 1⁹ ἔχρισέ σε ὁ Θεός . . . παρὰ τοὺς μετόχους σου.

c. In the Apostolic Fathers *cp.* —

Herm. *Past. Vis.* III 12 § 1 ἱλαρωτέραν παρὰ τὸ πρότερον, *Sim.* IX 18 § 2 πλείονα . . . παρά.   Barn. *Ep.* 4⁵ (in a quotation from Daniel which is neither O′ nor Θ) χαλεπώτερον παρὰ πάντα τὰ θήρια.

97. New Forms of Preposition. *a.* Besides the more liberal use made of the prepositions already current in classical Greek, we meet also in the LXX with new forms of preposition.

b. ἀπάνωθεν occurs in Swete's text in Jdg. 16²⁰: ii K. 11²⁰, ²⁴, 20²¹: iii K. 1⁵³: iv K. 2³. It not unnaturally gets confused in some places with the classical ἐπάνωθεν, which is very common in the LXX, having been found a convenient rendering of certain compound prepositions in the Hebrew.

c. ὑποκάτωθεν, which is only used as an adverb in classical Greek, assumes in the LXX the function of a preposition, *e.g.* —

Dt. 9¹⁴ ἐξαλείψω τὸ ὄνομα αὐτῶν ὑποκάτωθεν τοῦ οὐρανοῦ.

The corresponding form ὑπεράνωθεν occurs in the LXX only twice, once as an adverb in Ps. 77²³ and once as a preposition in —
Ezk. 1²⁵ ὑπεράνωθεν τοῦ στερεώματος.

d. ἔναντι, ἀπέναντι, and κατέναντι are prepositions unknown to classical authors, though ὑπέναντι is to be found in Polybius.

ἔναντι in many passages of the LXX has been replaced in Swete's text by ἐναντίον, but there are still numerous instances of it left, *e.g.* Ex. 28¹², ²³, ³⁴, 29¹⁰, ²³, ²⁴, ²⁵, ²⁶, ⁴². In N.T. it occurs in Lk. 1⁸, Acts 8²¹.

ἀπέναντι is also common, *e.g.* Gen. 3²⁴, 21²⁶, 23¹⁹, 25⁹, 49³⁰. In the N.T. it occurs in the sense of 'contrary to' in Acts 17⁷.

κατέναντι is specially frequent in the book of Sirach.

e. ἐνώπιον is another preposition unknown to classical authors, but extremely common in Biblical Greek, as being an apt equivalent for certain Hebrew forms of expression. Deissmann gives instances of its adverbial use in the Papyri, so that we need not suppose it to have been invented by the translators of the O.T. In the N.T. it occurs frequently in Luke-Acts, Paul, and Revelation, but is not used in Matthew or Mark.

κατενώπιον occurs in the LXX in Lvt. 4¹⁷: Josh. 1⁵, 3⁷, 21⁴⁴, 23⁹: Esther 5¹: Dan. Θ 5²². In N.T. in Eph. 1⁴: Col. 1²²: Jude²⁴.

f. ὀπίσω as a preposition is unclassical, but extremely common in the LXX.

In the N.T. it occurs in i Tim. 5¹⁵: Acts 5³⁷, 20³⁰: Mt. 4¹⁹, 10³⁸, 16²⁴: Lk. 14²⁷: Jn. 12¹⁹: Rev. 13³.

g. κατόπισθε(ν) is construed with a genitive in Hom. *Od.* XII 148, but its classical use is almost wholly adverbial, whereas in the LXX, in which it occurs twenty-four times in all, it is mainly prepositional.

In ii Chr. 34³⁸ we have ἀπὸ ὄπισθεν Κυρίου. *Cp.* Eccl. 1¹⁰ ἀπὸ ἐμπροσθεν ἡμῶν.

h. κυκλόθεν occurs in the LXX as a preposition in iii K. 18³²: Sir. 50¹² A: Jer. 17²⁶, 31¹⁷: i Mac. 14¹⁷.

In N.T. only in Rev. 4³, 5¹¹ κυκλόθεν τοῦ θρόνου.

κύκλῳ is sometimes used in the same way, as in iii K. 18³⁵: Sir. 23¹⁸: Is. 6²: Jer. 39⁴⁴.

Cp. Strabo XVII 6, p. 792 τὰ δὲ κύκλῳ τῆς κώμης.

i. Other prepositions that may be briefly noticed are ἐχόμενα πέτρας Ps. 140⁶, ἐσώτερον τῆς κολυμβήθρας Is. 22¹¹.

In Sir. 29²⁵ we have the combination καὶ πρὸς ἐπὶ τούτοις.

98. Prepositions after Verbs. The great use made of prepositions after verbs is one of the main characteristics of Biblical Greek. It is partly a feature of later Greek generally, but to a still greater extent it is due to the influence of the Hebrew. In the following list of instances perhaps the last only is irreproachable as Greek: —

ἀδυνατεῖν ἀπό Dt. 17[8].

ἀθετεῖν ἐν iv K. 1[1], 3[5, 7], 18[7], 24[1, 20]: ii Chr. 10[19].

αἱρετίζειν ἐν i Chr. 29[1]: ii Chr. 29[11].

βδελύσσεσθαι ἀπό Ex. 1[12].

βοᾶν ἐν iii K. 18[24].

ἐκδικεῖν ἐκ Dt. 18[19].

ἐκλέγειν ἐν i Chr. 28[5].

ἐλπίζειν ἐπί with accusative Ps. 4[6], 5[12], 9[11], 40[10].

ἐλπίζειν ἐπί with dative Ps. 7[1].

ἐνεδρεύειν ἐπί Jdg. 16[2].

ἐντρέπεσθαι ἀπό ii Chr. 36[12]: i Esd. 1[45].

ἐπικαλεῖσθαι ἐν iii K. 18[25, 26].

ἐσθίειν ἀπό Lvt. 22[6]: Jdg. 13[16].

εὐδοκεῖν ἐν Ps. 146[10].

θέλειν ἐν i K. 18[22]: i Chr. 28[4]: Ps. 146[10].

θεωρεῖν ἐν Jdg. 16[27].

καταφρονεῖν ἐπί Tobit 4[18].

λογίζεσθαι εἰς i K. 1[13].

μυκτηρίζειν ἐν i Esd. 1[51].

πατάσσειν ἐν ii. Chr. 28[5, 17].

ποιεῖν ἔλεος ἐν Josh. 2[12].

ποιεῖν ἔλεος μετά Jdg. 8[35].

πολεμεῖν ἐν i K. 28[15].

προσέχειν εἰς Ex. 9[21].

προσοχθίζειν ἀπό Nb. 22[3].

συνιέναι εἰς Ps. 27[5].

ὑπερηφανεύεσθαι ἀπό Tobit 4[14].

φείδεσθαι ἐπί Dt. 7[16].

φοβεῖσθαι ἀπό Dt. 1[20], 7[20]: Josh. 11[6]: iv K. 1[15]: Ps. 3[7].

φυλάσσεσθαι ἀπό Jdg. 13[14]. Cp. Xen. Cyrop. II 3 § 9, Hell. VII 2 § 10.

CONJUNCTIONS, 99–111

99. εἰ with the Subjunctive. *a.* In Homer εἰ, or its equivalent αἰ, is common with the subjunctive, especially when accompanied by κε(ν), *e.g. Il.* I 80, IV 249, VII 375, VIII 282, XI 791, XV 403, XVI 861, XVIII 601: *Od.* IV 35, V 471, 472, XVI 98, XXII 7.

In classical authors instances of εἰ with the subjunctive (without ἄν) are rare rather than absent. Some of them may have been improved out of existence, owing to a desire for uniformity.

Plato *Laws* 761 C εἴ τί που ἄλσος . . . ἀνειμένον ᾖ. Xen. *Anab.* III 2 § 22 οἱ πόταμοι, εἰ καὶ πρόσω τῶν πηγῶν ἄποροι ὦσι. Soph. *Ant.* 710 κεἴ τις ᾖ σοφός. See GMT. 454.

b. In Hellenistic Greek the use of εἰ with the subjunctive becomes common, *e.g.* —

Arist. *E.E.* II 1 § 17 εἰ ᾖ ἄνθρωπος, 8 § 9 εἴ τις προσθῇ, 18 εἰ γὰρ . . . ἀποκτείνῃ, 10 § 21 εἰ πολεμῶσιν. Philo II 19, *De Abr.* § 25 εἰ ἔμμισθος ᾖ. Jos. *B.J.* I 31 § 1 εἰ . . . ἀσθενήσῃ, *Ant.* I 2 § 3 εἰ καὶ συμβῇ.

We should therefore antecedently expect to find this construction in the LXX, and yet it is seldom found. It occurs in Jdg. 11[9], where an indicative and subjunctive are both made dependent on εἰ — εἰ ἐπιστρέφετέ με ὑμεῖς παρατάξασθαι ἐν υἱοῖς Ἀμμὼν καὶ παραδῷ Κύριος αὐτοὺς ἐνώπιον ἐμοῦ. In Dt. 8[5] Swete's text has παιδεύσαι in place of παιδεύσῃ. In i K. 14[37] εἰ καταβῶ ὀπίσω τῶν ἀλλοφύλων is so punctuated as to become an instance of εἰ interrogative (§ 100). In Sirach 22[26] εἰ κακά μοι συμβῇ, the συμβῇ has given place to συμβήσεται.

In the N.T. there are a few instances of εἰ with the subjunctive — Rom. 11[14] εἴ πως παραζηλώσω. Phil. 3[11] εἴ πως καταντήσω εἰς τὴν ἐξανάστασιν, 3[12] εἰ καὶ καταλάβω.

100. εἰ Interrogative. *a.* In classical Greek εἰ is often used in indirect questions, *e.g.* —

Thuc. I 5 § 2 ἐρωτῶντες εἰ λῃσταί εἰσιν. Plat. *Apol.* 21 D ἤρετο γὰρ δή, εἴ τις ἐμοῦ εἴη σοφώτερος. Xen. *Anab.* I 10 § 5 ἐβουλεύετο . . . εἰ πέμποιέν τινας ἢ πάντες ἴοιεν.

b. In Biblical Greek εἰ has become a direct interrogative particle. This transition seems so natural as to make us doubt the statement of Jannaris (*Hist. Gk. Gr.* § 2055) that εἰ is in all these cases 'nothing but an itacistic misspelling for the colloquial ᾖ.' In

Gen. 43[7] λέγων Εἰ ἔτι ὁ πατὴρ ὑμῶν ζῇ; εἰ ἔστιν ὑμῖν ἀδελφός; . . . μὴ ᾔδειμεν εἰ ἐρεῖ ἡμῖν κτλ.

we have first the direct and then the indirect use of εἰ as an interrogative particle. For other instances of the former take —

i K. 15[32] καὶ εἶπεν Ἀγάγ Εἰ οὕτως πικρὸς ὁ θάνατος; ii K. 20[17] καὶ εἶπεν ἡ γυνή Εἰ σὺ εἶ Ἰωάβ; iii K. 20[20] καὶ εἶπεν Ἀχαὰβ πρὸς

Ἠλειού Εἰ εὕρηκάς με, ὁ ἐχθρός μου;   Cp. also Gen. 17¹⁷, 39⁸, 43²⁷:
Ex. 2¹⁴: Jdg. 13¹¹: i K. 9¹¹, 10²², ²⁴, 14³⁷, ⁴⁵, 15²²: iii K. 13¹⁴, 18¹⁷:
iv K. 1³: Tob. 5⁵: Jonah 4⁴, ⁹: Joel 1²: Dan. 6²⁰.

c. The interrogative εἰ is sometimes followed by the deliberative conjunctive, e.g. —

> Jdg. 20²⁸ Εἰ προσθῶμεν ἔτι ἐξελθεῖν;   ii K. 2¹ Εἰ ἀναβῶ εἰς μίαν τῶν πόλεων Ἰούδα;   i Chr. 14¹⁰ Εἰ ἀναβῶ ἐπὶ τοὺς ἀλλοφύλους;

d. In the N.T. εἰ interrogative is of common occurrence —

> Mk. 8²³ ἐπηρώτα αὐτόν, Εἴ τι βλέπεις;   Cp. Mk. 10², where the question may be either direct or indirect.   Mt. 12¹⁰ ἐπηρώτησαν αὐτὸν λέγοντες, Εἰ ἔξεστι τοῖς σάββασι θεραπεύειν;   Cp. Mt. 19³.   Lk. 13²³ Κύριε, εἰ ὀλίγοι οἱ σωζόμενοι;   Cp. Lk. 22⁴⁹. Acts 1⁶ Κύριε, εἰ ἐν τῷ χρόνῳ τούτῳ κτλ.   Cp. Acts 7¹, 19², 21³⁷, 22²⁵, 23⁹.

101. εἰ in Oaths.   a.   εἰ is often found in the LXX after an oath in a sense practically equivalent to a negative, e.g. —

> Ps. 94¹¹ ὡς ὤμοσα ἐν τῇ ὀργῇ μου Εἰ ἐλεύσονται εἰς τὴν κατάπουσίν μου.

This use of εἰ is a sheer Hebraism. The negative force imported into εἰ is due to a suppression of the apodosis, which the reader may supply as his own sense of reverence suggests. Other instances will be found in Gen. 14²³: Nb. 32¹⁰, ¹¹: Dt. 1³⁴, ³⁵: i K. 3¹⁴, 14⁴⁵, 17⁵⁵, 19⁶, 28¹⁰: ii K. 19³⁵: iii K. 1⁵², 2⁸, 17¹, ¹², 18¹⁰: iv K. 2²: Ps. 131²⁻⁴: Jer. 45¹⁶.

b. When an affirmative asseveration is conveyed by the oath, it is introduced by ὅτι, not by εἰ, as in —

> i K. 29⁶ ζῇ Κύριος, ὅτι εὐθὴς σὺ καὶ ἀγαθὸς ἐν ὀφθαλμοῖς μου,
> iii K. 18¹⁵ ζῇ Κύριος . . . ὅτι σήμερον ὀφθήσομαι σοι,

or else is devoid of a conjunction, as in —

> i K. 1²⁶ ζῇ ἡ ψυχή σου, ἐγὼ ἡ γυνὴ κτλ.   Jdg. 8¹⁹ ζῇ Κύριος, εἰ ἐζωογονήκειτε αὐτούς, οὐκ ἂν ἀπέκτεινα ὑμᾶς.

c. In iv K. 3¹⁴ ὅτι εἰ μή is merely a strengthened form of εἰ μή, so that the ἢ by which it is followed in Swete's text, instead of εἰ, seems to destroy the sense.

d. In the N.T. we have the jurative use of εἰ in —

> Mk. 8¹² ἀμὴν λέγω ὑμῖν, εἰ δοθήσεται τῇ γενεᾷ ταύτῃ σημεῖον.

Also in Hb. 3¹¹, 4³ in quotations from Ps. 94¹¹.

102. εἰ μή in Oaths. As εἰ assumes a negative force in oaths and asseverations, so on the same principle εἰ μή becomes positive. Instances are —

Nb. 14³⁵ ἐγὼ Κύριος ἐλάλησα, εἰ μὴ οὕτως ποιήσω (= I will do so). Is. 45²³ κατ᾽ ἐμαυτοῦ ὀμνύω, εἰ μὴ ἐξελεύσεται ἐκ τοῦ στόματός μου δικαιοσύνη (= righteousness shall go forth from my mouth).

In iii K. 21²³ ἐὰν δὲ πολεμήσομεν αὐτοὺς κατ᾽ εὐθύ, εἰ μὴ κραταιώσομεν ὑπὲρ αὐτούς the oath itself is suppressed as well as the apodosis.

103. εἰ μήν. εἰ μήν as a formula of asseveration has been supposed to be a blend between the Hebraistic εἰ μή (§ 102) and the Greek ἦ μήν. It is however not confined to Biblical Greek, but occurs also on the Papyri. We treat it under the head of Conjunctions because of the lack of accent. It would perhaps be more correct to write it εἶ μήν and regard it as an Interjection. The following are all the passages in which it occurs in the LXX —

Gen. 22¹⁷ εἰ μὴν εὐλογῶν εὐλογήσω σε, 42¹⁵ νὴ τὴν ὑγίαν Φαραώ, εἰ μὴν κατάσκοποί ἐστε. Nb. 14²³, ²⁸: Jdg. 15⁷: Job 1¹¹, 2⁵, 27³: Judith 1¹²: Baruch 2²⁹: Ezk. 33²⁷, 34⁸, 36⁵, 38¹⁹.

In ii K. 19³⁵ what we have is εἰ interrogative (§ 100) followed by μήν.

In the N.T. εἰ μήν occurs only in Hb. 6¹⁴ in a quotation from Gen. 22¹⁷.

104. ἐάν, etc., with the Indicative. *a.* As in Hellenistic Greek εἰ may take the subjunctive, so on the other hand ἐάν, ὅταν and the like are found with the indicative.

Instances of ἐάν with the indicative in the LXX are —

Gen. 44³⁰ ἐὰν εἰσπορεύομαι. Jdg. 6³ ἐὰν ἔσπειραν. iii K. 21²³ ἐὰν δὲ πολεμήσομεν αὐτοὺς κατ᾽ εὐθύ. Job 22³ ἐὰν σὺ ἦσθα.

So in N.T. —

i Jn. 5¹⁵ ἐὰν οἴδαμεν. Acts 7⁷ τὸ ἔθνος, ᾧ ἐὰν δουλεύσουσι. *Cp.* Herm. *Past. Vis.* III 12 § 3 ἐὰν . . . εἰρηνεύετε, I 3 § 2 ἐὰν . . . μετανοήσουσιν.

b. Instances of ὅταν with the indicative in the LXX are —

Gen. 38⁹ ὅταν εἰσήρχετο. Ex. 17¹¹ ὅταν ἐπῆρεν Μωυσῆς τὰς χεῖρας. Nb. 11⁹ καὶ ὅταν κατέβη ἡ δρόσος, 21⁹ ὅταν ἔδακνεν ὄφις ἄνθρωπον. i K. 17³⁴ ὅταν ἤρχετο ὁ λέων καὶ ἡ ἄρκος. Ps. 119⁷ ὅταν ἐλάλουν αὐτοῖς.

c. So in N.T. —

Mk. 3¹¹ καὶ τὰ πνεύματα τὰ ἀκάθαρτα, ὅταν αὐτὸν ἐθεώρει, προσέπιπτεν αὐτῷ, 11¹⁹ ὅταν ὀψὲ ἐγένετο.   Rev. 8¹ ὅταν ἤνοιξε.
Cp. Barn. *Ep.* 4¹⁴ ὅταν βλέπετε, 15⁵ ὅταν . . . καταργήσει.   Ign.
Eph. 8¹ ὅταν γὰρ μηδεμία ἔρις ἐνήρεισται ἐν ὑμῖν.   Herm. *Past.*
Sim. IX 1 § 6 ὅταν ὁ ἥλιος ἐπικεκαύκει, ξηραὶ ἐγένοντο, 4 § 5 ὅταν
. . . ἐτέθησαν.   *Cp.* 17 § 3.   6 § 4 ὅταν ἐπάτασσεν.

d. Under the same head come the following —

Ex. 33⁸, 34³⁴ ἡνίκα δ᾽ ἂν εἰσεπορεύετο Μωσῆς, 40³⁰ ἡνίκα δ᾽ ἂν ἀνέβη
ἀπὸ τῆς σκηνῆς ἡ νεφέλη.   Tobit 7¹¹ ὁπότε ἐὰν εἰσεπορεύοντο.
Cp. Barn. *Ep.* 12³ ὁπόταν καθεῖλεν.

105. ἐάν after a Relative. *a.* ἐάν for ἄν after a relative seems to
occur occasionally in Mss. of Attic authors, especially of Xenophon,
but to have been expunged by editors. It is proved by the Papyri to
have been in common use in Egypt during the first two centuries B.C.
Biblical Greek is so full of this usage that it is superfluous to col-
lect examples. Besides the simple relative in its various cases we
have —

ὅσα ἐάν Gen. 44¹ : Ex. 13¹².   ἡνίκα ἐάν Gen. 24⁴¹ : Ex. 13⁵.
οὗ ἐάν Ex. 20²⁴.   καθὼς ἐάν Sir. 14¹¹ : Dan. O' 1¹³.
ὅθεν ἐάν Ex. 5¹¹.

As a rule the subjunctive follows, but not always.

Gen. 2¹⁹ πᾶν ὃ ἐὰν ἐκάλεσεν.

b. The use of ἄν in such cases is not quite excluded, *e.g.* Ex. 12¹⁵, ¹⁹ :
Nb. 22²⁰.

c. In the N.T. also it is easier to find ἐάν in this connexion than
ἄν, *e.g.* —

ὃς ἐάν Mt. 5¹⁹, 10¹⁴, ⁴² : Lk. 17³³.
ᾧ ἐάν Mt. 11²⁷ : Lk. 10²².
οὓς ἐάν i Cor. 16³.
ὃ ἐάν i Cor. 6¹⁸ : Gal. 6⁷ : Col. 3²³ : Eph. 6⁸ : Jn. 15⁷ : i Jn. 3²² :
    iii Jn.⁵
καθὸ ἐάν ii Cor. 8¹².
ὅπου ἐάν Mt. 8¹⁹.
ὅ τι ἐάν i Jn. 3¹⁹.

For instances of ἄν take i Jn. 3¹⁷ : Mt. 10¹¹ : Lk. 10⁵, ⁸, ¹⁰, ³⁵.

d. In the Apostolic Fathers also we find the same use of ἐάν after relatives —

Barn. *Ep.* 7¹¹ ὃς ἐὰν θέλῃ, 11⁸ πᾶν ῥῆμα ὃ ἐὰν ἐξελεύσεται. Herm. *Past. Vis.* III 2 § 1 ὃς ἐὰν πάθῃ, *Sim.* VII 7 ὅσοι [ἐὰν] ἐν ταῖς ἐντολαῖς μου ταύταις πορευθῶσιν, IX 2 § 7 ὅσα ἐάν σοι δείξω.

106. ἵνα with the Indicative. *a.* In the vast majority of places in which ἵνα occurs in the LXX it governs the subjunctive. The optative, as we have seen, has practically vanished from dependent clauses. But there are a few passages in Swete's text, and perhaps Ms. authority for more, in which ἵνα after a primary tense or the imperative mood takes a future indicative.

Gen. 16² εἴσελθε . . . ἵνα τεκνοποιήσεις. iii K. 2³ φυλάξεις . . . ἵνα ποιήσεις. Sus. O′²⁸ ἐνεδρεύοντες ἵνα θανατώσουσιν αὐτήν. Dan. O′ 3⁹⁶ ἐγὼ κρίνω ἵνα πᾶν ἔθνος . . . διαμελισθήσεται.

b. The 1st person singular of the 1st aorist subjunctive may possibly have served as a stepping-stone to this use. Take for instance —

ii K. 19²² ἀπόστηθι . . . ἵνα μὴ πατάξω σε.

This might easily lead by false analogy to —

ἀπελεύσομαι, ἵνα μὴ πατάξεις με.

This theory however fails to account for the following —

i Esd. 4⁵⁰ ἵνα ἀφίουσι. Tob. 14⁹ σὺ δὲ τήρησον τὸν νόμον . . . ἵνα σοι καλῶς ἦν.

The last can only be regarded as a monstrosity.

c. In the N.T. ἵνα with the future indicative occurs occasionally and is common in Revelation —

i Cor. 9¹⁸ ἵνα . . . θήσω. Gal. 2⁴ ἵνα ἡμᾶς καταδουλώσουσιν. i Pet. 3¹ ἵνα . . . κερδηθήσονται. Rev. 3⁹, 6⁴, 8³, 9²⁰, 14¹³, 22²⁴ ἵνα ἔσται . . . καὶ . . . εἰσελθωσιν.

The last instance shows that even in the debased Greek of this book the subjunctive still claimed its rights on occasions.

d. There are two apparent instances in St. Paul's writings of ἵνα with a present indicative —

i Cor. 4⁶ ἵνα μὴ . . . φυσιοῦσθε. Gal. 1¹⁷ ἵνα αὐτοὺς ζηλοῦτε.

With regard to these Winer came to the conclusion that 'ἵνα with the indicative present is to be regarded as an impropriety of later

Greek.' Perhaps however in these cases it is the accidence, not the syntax, that is astray, φυσιοῦσθε and ζηλοῦτε being meant for the subjunctive. Winer closes his discussion of the subject by saying, 'It is worthy of remark, however the case may be, that in both instances the verb ends in οω.' Here the true explanation seems to lie. The hypothesis of an irregular contraction is not in itself a violent one, and it is confirmed by a passage of the LXX —

Ex. 1¹⁶ ὅταν μαιοῦσθε τὰς Ἑβραίας καὶ ὦσιν πρὸς τῷ τίκτειν.

107. Ellipse before ὅτι. By the suppression of an imperative of a verb of knowing ὅτι acquires the sense of 'know that.'

Ex. 3¹² λέγων ῞Οτι ἔσομαι μετὰ σοῦ.   Jdg. 15⁷ εἶπεν . . . Σαμψών
. . . ὅτι εἰ μὴν ἐκδικήσω ἐν ὑμῖν.   iii K. 19² εἶπεν . . . ὅτι ταύτην τὴν ὥραν κτλ.

This usage originates in the Hebrew, but has a parallel in Greek in the similar ellipse before ὡς, which is common in Euripides, e.g. Med. 609: Alc. 1094: Phœn. 720, 1664: Ion 935, 1404: Hel. 126, 831: Hec. 346, 400. Cp. Soph. Aj. 39.

108. ἀλλ᾽ ἤ. a. The combination of particles ἀλλ᾽ ἤ occurs in Swete's text 114 times at least. In most of these passages ἀλλ᾽ ἤ is simply a strengthened form of ἀλλά. If it differs at all from it, it is in the same way as 'but only' in English differs from the simple 'but.' In the remainder of the 114 passages ἀλλ᾽ ἤ has the same force as the English 'but' in the sense of 'except' after a negative expressed or implied. It is thus an equivalent for the classical εἰ μή. But even this latter meaning can be borne by the simple ἀλλά, if we may trust the reading of —

Gen. 21²⁶ οὐδὲ ἐγὼ ἤκουσα ἀλλὰ σήμερον.

b. The idea has been entertained that ἀλλ᾽ ἤ is not for ἀλλὰ ἤ, as the accentuation assumes, but for ἄλλο ἤ. This view would suit very well with such passages as Gen. 28¹⁷, 47¹⁸: Dt. 10¹²: ii K. 12³: Sir. 22¹⁴, where it happens that a neuter singular precedes, but it seems to have nothing else to recommend it.

Where ἀλλ᾽ ἤ follows ἄλλος or ἕτερος, as in iv K. 5¹⁷: Dan. 3⁹⁵, Θ 2¹¹: i Mac. 10³⁸, the ἀλλά would be superfluous in classical Greek, so that in these cases it might be thought that the ἤ was strengthened by the ἀλλά, and not *vice versa*: but if we accept the use in Gen. 21²⁶, it follows that even here it is the ἀλλά which is strengthened.

c. In contrast with the abundance of instances in the O.T. and in

Hellenistic Greek generally, *e.g.* in Aristotle, it is strange how rare this combination is in the N.T. In the Revisers' text it occurs only twice— Lk. 12⁵¹ οὐχί, λέγω ὑμῖν, ἀλλ᾽ ἢ διαμερισμόν. ii Cor. 1¹³ οὐ γὰρ ἄλλα γράφομεν ὑμῖν, ἀλλ᾽ ἢ ἃ ἀναγινώσκετε.

109. ὅτι ἀλλ᾽ ἤ. This combination of particles occurs in the following passages of the LXX — Jdg. 15¹³ : i K. 2³⁰, 21⁴, 21⁶, 30¹⁷, 30²² : ii K. 13³³, 21² : iii K. 18¹⁸ : iv K. 4², 5¹⁵, 10²³, 14⁶, 17³⁵, ³⁶, 23²³ : ii Chr. 2⁶.

An examination of these instances will show that they all fall under the same two heads as ἀλλ᾽ ἤ. In the bulk of them ὅτι ἀλλ᾽ ἤ is simply a strongly adversative particle (= but); in the remainder it is like our 'but' = 'except' after a negative expressed or implied. The reader will observe that the range of literature, within which this combination of particles is found, is very limited, being almost confined to the four books of Kingdoms. It looks therefore as if we had here a mere device of translation, not any recognised usage of later Greek. In all but the first two instances the underlying Hebrew is the same, consisting of two particles; in the first two there is only the particle corresponding to ὅτι, and these passages seem really to fall under § 107.

There is one place in which we find this combination of particles still more complicated by the use of διότι in place of ὅτι.

iii K. 22¹⁸ Οὐκ εἶπα πρὸς σέ Οὐ προφητεύει οὗτός μοι καλά, διότι ἀλλ᾽ ἢ κακά;

110. ὅτι εἰ μή. This combination occurs in the following passages —

ii K. 2²⁷ Ζῇ Κύριος, ὅτι εἰ μὴ ἐλάλησας, διότι τότε ἐκ πρωίθεν ἀνέβη ὁ λαός. iii K. 17¹ Ζῇ Κύριος . . . εἰ ἔσται . . . ὑετός· ὅτι εἰ μὴ διὰ στόματος λόγου μου. iv K. 3¹⁴ Ζῇ Κύριος . . . ὅτι εἰ μὴ πρόσωπον Ἰωσαφὰθ . . . ἐγὼ λαμβάνω, εἰ (A) ἐπέβλεψα πρὸς σέ.

In the first of the above passages 'unless,' in the second 'except,' in the third 'only that' seem to give the exact shade of meaning. In all of them the ὅτι might be dispensed with, and owes its presence to the Hebrew.

111. ἀλλ᾽ ἢ ὅτι. There are four passages in which this combination occurs —

Nb. 13²⁹ ἀλλ᾽ ἢ ὅτι θρασὺ τὸ ἔθνος. i K. 10¹⁹ Οὐχί, ἀλλ᾽ ἢ ὅτι βασιλέα στήσεις ἐφ᾽ ἡμῶν, 12¹² Οὐχί, ἀλλ᾽ ἢ ὅτι βασιλεὺς βασιλεύσει ἐφ᾽ ἡμῶν. ii K. 19²⁸ ὅτι οὐκ ἦν πᾶς ὁ οἶκος τοῦ πατρός μου ἀλλ᾽ ἢ ὅτι ἄνδρες θανάτου.

No one meaning suits all the above passages. In the first of them the Hebrew which corresponds to ἀλλ' ἢ ὅτι is rendered in the R.V. 'howbeit.' In the next two ἀλλ' ἢ ὅτι might just as well have been ὅτι ἀλλ' ἤ (= Lat. *sed*), as in Jdg. 15³ (§ 109). In the fourth also ὅτι ἀλλ' ἤ might have been used in the sense of 'but' in 'nothing but,' *etc.*, as in i K. 21⁶, 30¹⁷: iv K. 4², 5¹⁵: ii Chr. 2⁶.

112. λέγων, etc., for the Hebrew Gerund. *a.* A special cause of irregularity in LXX Greek is the treatment of the Hebrew gerund of the verb 'to say' (= Lat. *dicendo*), which is constantly used to introduce speeches. As the Greek language has no gerund, this is rendered in the LXX by a participle. But the form being fixed in the Hebrew, the tendency is to keep it so in the Greek also. Hence it is quite the exception to find the participle agreeing with its subject, as in —

i K. 19² ἀπήγγειλεν . . . λέγων, 19¹¹ ἀπήγγειλε . . . λέγουσα.

b. If the subject is neuter or feminine, the participle may still be masculine —

Gen. 15¹: i K. 15¹⁰ ἐγενήθη ῥῆμα Κυρίου . . . λέγων. iv K. 18³⁶ ὅτι ἐντολὴ τοῦ βασιλέως λέγων.

Also, if the sentence is impersonal —

iii K. 20⁹ ἐγέγραπτο . . λέγων. ii Chr. 21¹² ἦλθεν . . . ἐν γραφῇ . . . λέγων. Jonah 3⁷ ἐρρέθη . . . λέγων.

c. But the participle may even refer to another subject, as —

iv K. 19⁹ ἤκουσεν . . . λέγων = he heard say.

d. It is rare for the Greek to fare so well as in —

Dt. 13¹² ἐὰν δὲ ἀκούσῃς . . . λεγόντων.

And here the genitive is probably not governed by ἀκούειν, but used absolutely. *Cp.* —

i K. 24² ἀπηγγέλη αὐτῷ λεγόντων.

e. A very common case is to have the verb in the passive, either impersonally or personally, and the participle in the nominative plural masculine, thus —

ἀπηγγέλη . . . λέγοντες Gen. 38²⁴, 48²: Josh. 2², 10¹⁷: i K. 14³³, 15¹², 19¹⁹, 23¹.
ἀνηγγέλη . . . λέγοντες Jdg. 16²: Gen. 22²⁰.
διεβοήθη ἡ φωνὴ . . . λέγοντες Gen. 45¹⁶.
εὐλογηθήσεται Ἰσραὴλ λέγοντες Gen. 48²⁰.

An adjacent case is —

Ezk. 12²² Τίς ἡ παραβολὴ ὑμῖν . . . λέγοντες;

f. When the verb is active and finite, the construction presents itself as good Greek, as in —

iii K. 12¹⁰ ἐλάλησαν . . . λέγοντες,

but this is little better than an accident, for what immediately follows is —

Τάδε λαλήσεις τῷ λαῷ τούτῳ τοῖς λαλήσασι πρὸς σὲ λέγοντες κτλ.

In Dt. 18¹⁶ we have even ᾐτήσω . . . λέγοντες.

g. Where the principal verb is not one of saying, the divorce between it and the participle is complete, both in sense and grammar —

Ex. 5¹⁴ ἐμαστιγώθησαν . . . λέγοντες, 5¹⁹ ἑώρων . . . λέγοντες,

where the 'being beaten' and the 'seeing' are predicated of one set of persons and the 'saying' of another. *Cp.* the complex case in i Mac. 13¹⁷, ¹⁸.

h. In the N.T. this Hebraism occurs only once —

Rev. 11¹⁵ φωναὶ . . . λέγοντες.

113. Idiomatic Use of προστιθέναι. *a.* Another very common Hebraism is the use of προστιθέναι with the infinitive of another verb in the sense of doing a thing more or again, *e.g.* —

Gen. 37⁸ προσέθεντο ἔτι μισεῖν = they hated still more. *Cp.* Gen. 4², ¹², 8²¹, 44²³. Ex. 8²⁹ μὴ προσθῇς ἔτι . . . ἐξαπατῆσαι. *Cp.* Ex. 9²⁸, 10²⁸, 14¹³. Nb. 22¹⁵, ¹⁹, ²⁵: Dt. 3²⁶, 5²⁵: Josh. 7¹²: Jdg. 8²⁸, 10⁶, 13¹, ²¹: i Mac. 9¹.

b. Sometimes τοῦ precedes the infinitive, as —

Ex. 9³⁴ προσέθετο τοῦ ἁμαρτάνειν. Josh. 23¹³ οὐ μὴ προσθῇ Κύριος τοῦ ἐξολεθρεῦσαι. Jdg. 2²¹ οὐ προσθήσω τοῦ ἐξᾶραι. *Cp.* Jdg. 9³⁷, 10¹³.

c. The same construction may be used impersonally in the passive —

Ex. 5⁷ οὐκέτι προστεθήσεται διδόναι ἄχυρον τῷ λαῷ.

d. Sometimes the dependent verb is dropped after the middle or passive —

Nb. 22²⁶ καὶ προσέθετο ὁ ἄγγελος τοῦ θεοῦ καὶ ἀπελθὼν ὑπέστη. *Cp.* iv K. 1¹¹. Ex. 11⁶ ἥτις τοιαύτη οὐ γέγονεν καὶ τοιαύτη οὐκέτι προστεθήσεται.